INDIA
PAKISTAN
BANGLADESH

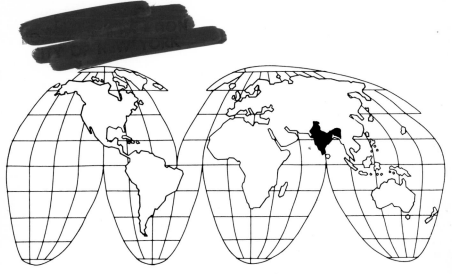

HISTORY, CULTURE, PEOPLE

MILTON JAY BELASCO
Chairman, Department of Social Studies
William Howard Taft High School, New York

HAROLD E. HAMMOND
Professor of History
Formerly Associate Dean, College of
Arts and Sciences, New York University

Globe Book Company

Englewood Cliffs, New Jersey

Series Consultant
HAROLD E. HAMMOND, Ph.D.

THE REGIONAL STUDIES SERIES
Africa
China
India-Pakistan-Bangladesh
Japan-Korea-Taiwan
Latin America
The Middle East
Southeast Asia
The Soviet Union

REVISED EDITION

Second Edition 1985

ISBN: 0-87065-631-7

Printed in the United States of America   9   8

INTRODUCTION

When people think of the Indian subcontinent the images that come to mind are perhaps the Taj Mahal, famine and overpopulation, women wearing *saris,* the influence of British colonialism, and Mahatma Gandhi—the "father of modern India." But these images are only part of the picture, a glimpse of the lands and peoples that are India, Pakistan, and Bangladesh.

In this region are over 800 million people with a shared history but vastly different cultural and religious backgrounds. In some ways the history of the Indian subcontinent matches and surpasses that of Europe in its cultural and social achievements. Its rich religious and artistic heritage can be traced back nearly 3000 years. In fact, consciousness of the past has inspired the peoples of this region in their quest for independence. The spirit of nationalism led to freedom from British rule in 1947, when the nations of India and Pakistan were formed. That same spirit and national pride resulted in the creation of the new nation of Bangladesh after one of the most bloody civil wars in modern history.

Family customs and social patterns in this region are founded on centuries old traditions. Largely an agricultural region, the people who live in villages retain many of their ancestors' practices. Yet many of these farming communities have adjusted to the demands for increased productivity by adopting new scientific methods and modern equipment. In the rapidly expanding urban centers, people work in modern industries and businesses. They face the same problems of inadequate housing, poverty, unemployment, and crime that plague American cities. These urban dwellers are also incorporating new lifestyles and customs into their daily lives that reflect global interests as well as the growing involvement of these nations in world affairs.

SOVIET UNION

MONGOLIA

C H I N A

HINDU
KUSH

Khyber Pass

Kashmir

Kabul ★

★ Islamabad
Rawalpindi

AFGHANISTAN

Lahore

Lyallpur

T I B E T

Himalaya

BHUTAN

PAKISTAN

Indus R.

New Delhi ★

Thar Desert

Mountains

NEPAL

Brahmaputra R.

Kanpur

Ganges R.

Dacca
★

Hyderabad

I N D I A

Khulna

BURMA

Karachi

Calcutta

Chittagong

Ahmadabad

Vindhya Mts.

BANGLADESH

Narbada R.

Tapti R.

Bay of
Bengal

Rangoon ★

Arabian Sea

Bombay

Deccan

Hyderabad

Godavari R.

Eastern Ghats

Western Ghats

Plateau

Krishna R.

Madras

Bangalore

N

Cauvery R.

W   E

S

Cape Comorin

SRI LANKA

0   Miles   500

Colombo ★

0   Kilometers   804

INDIAN OCEAN

India Pakistan
Bangladesh

CONTENTS

THE INDIAN SUBCONTINENT: LAND AND PEOPLES 1

A. THE LAND

The subcontinent of India is in South Asia. It is called a sub-continent because of its size, its topographical features and its location to the rest of Asia.

India is shaped like a huge triangle. The broad northern top of the triangle is separated from the rest of Asia by the towering, snow-covered Himalaya Mountains. (In fact, the word "Himalaya" means "home of snow.") The point of the triangle juts into the Indian Ocean on the south.

In the north, India's neighbors are Communist China and Tibet (controlled by China), and the two small countries of Nepal and Bhutan. In the east, India has a long border with Bangladesh and yet another with Burma. On the west side, Pakistan borders India from the coast north to Kashmir. The tip of the triangle, Cape Comorin, with the Arabian Sea on the west, and the Bay of Bengal on the east, is separated by about 70 miles from the island of Sri Lanka.

India has a land border nearly 9500 miles long, and a sea-coast of over 3500 miles. Its vast area makes it the seventh largest country in the world. The Indian subcontinent is so large that all the countries of Western Europe could fit comfortably within it. India covers about 1,270,000 square miles—about one-third the size of the United States. But there are over 626 million people, almost three times the number in the United States. India is the second most populous nation in the world; only China has a larger population.

It is important to note that, until late 1971, there were two parts of Pakistan which were separated by nearly 1,000 miles of India. Both had originally been part of India until the partition in 1947. In Chapter 8 we will study the circumstances of their separation into two independent Muslim nations, Pakistan and the new nation of Bangladesh. Geographically, however, we will consider India, Pakistan, and Bangladesh together.

Geographic Areas of India. The lofty Himalayas on the northern border of India slope into jungle-covered hills which descend into a great plain that spreads from east to west across the broad part of the triangle. The southern part of this great plain extends to the Vindhya Mountains which slope into a great plateau. This flat tableland is separated from the sea by mountain ranges on the east and west. Between the mountains and the coast there are broad coastal plains. Thus, the subcontinent of India is divided into four major geographical areas:
1. The Himalaya Mountain area
2. The Ganges (lowland) plain
3. The Deccan plateau
4. The Southern coastal plains

The Himalayan Mountain Area. The most impressive geographic feature of India is the great Himalayan Mountain Range. It stretches across the top of India in a curve that is more than 1500 miles long and 150 to 200 miles wide. It forms a natural boundary for India.

The mountains create a wall that averages over 17,000 feet high. There are many mountain peaks that rise to 25,000 feet; the tallest is Mt. Everest (at the Nepal-Tibet border), 29,028 feet. Travel across the mountains is very difficult. There are no railroads, and flying across the mountains is very dangerous. There are a few passes in the western part of the mountain range through which foreign peoples have invaded India. The most famous of these is the Khyber Pass, which is now in the nation of Pakistan.

The mountains are very important for three other reasons:
1. They block the cold winds that blow southward out of Tibet and central Asia, and thus protect northern India from frost and freezing cold.
2. The Indian subcontinent's main rivers have their sources in the Himalayas. The Ganges, the Jumna, the Indus, the Brahmapu-

tra and their branches, all rise in these mountains. They receive a steady supply of water from the melting snows and glaciers of the Himalayas. They do not depend on rainfall. This is vital to the millions of people who live in the northern plains that are watered by these rivers.

3. The Himalayan wall has an important effect on the Indian monsoon winds that blow northeastward from the Indian Ocean until they hit the mountains. The winds rise and cool off, and the water vapor forms rain that falls on the lowland plains. (We shall see the importance of the monsoons on Indian life later in this chapter.)

The mountains taper down in the east to the steaming jungles of Assam and to the burning Thar Desert in the west. Thus, the mountains, the desert, and the jungle, sprawling across the top of the Indian triangle from west to east, have cut India off from the rest of Asia.

The Lowland Plain. The mountains slope gradually into the Ganges plain which stretches for 2000 miles across India and into Bangladesh. This flat, fertile land is watered by the great rivers of India—the Ganges, the Brahmaputra, the Indus and their tributaries. The plain is about 200 miles wide, and forms one of the largest areas of farmland in the world. It is known as "the breadbasket of India."

The continual deposits of rich topsoil (alluvium) brought down from the mountains by the rivers make the plain fertile. Rainfall here averages from 40 to 80 inches a year.

Nearly two-thirds of the Indian people live in this area. Here are found more of India's villages, more irrigated, productive land, and more industry than anywhere else in India. Half of India's big cities are located here.

The Deccan Plateau. The Vindhya Range is the southern limit of this great plain. These mountains separate the lowland plains from a large plateau known as the Deccan. This broad, flat tableland is from 1000 to 3000 feet above sea level, and almost fills the Indian peninsula.

This region is cut off from the Arabian Sea on the west and the Bay of Bengal on the east by two rugged mountain ranges—the Western and Eastern Ghats which run parallel to the coasts. ("Ghat" means "high or elevated place.") The Western Ghats, with 7000-foot peaks, rise abruptly about 30 miles inland from the seacoast. They are very difficult to climb, and there are only a few passes in their unbroken 800-mile length. The Eastern Ghats are lower; the mountains average about 2000 feet high.

The Ghats are high enough to prevent the summer monsoons from bringing adequate rain to much of the Deccan plateau. Rain, falling generally during the summer months, varies from 20 to 40 inches. Alluvial deposits are not left by the rivers that flow through this region. In fact, many of these rivers dry up during periods of drought. Much of India's mineral wealth is found in the Deccan plateau.

The Southern Coastal Plains. Fertile, alluvial plains stretch along both coasts of the peninsula between the Ghats and the sea. In these long coastal plains, rainfall varies between 80 and 200 inches a year. Population density is very high in these areas of heavy rains, warm climate and fertile soil. More people per square mile live along the western Malabar coast than in the whole Ganges valley.

B. CLIMATE

Within the vast area of the region, climate varies from the bitter cold of the Himalayas to the hot, steaming humidity of the jungles; from the parched dryness of the western Thar Desert to the soggy wetness of eastern Assam. The climate the Indians enjoy and endure depends upon where they live in India.

In India and Bangladesh, there are only three seasons each year; the hot and rainy season, the cool season, and the dry season. The seasons follow the changing monsoons which have such a great influence on the life of the people.

When it is hot, it is *very* hot. When it is cold, it is very un-

CLIMATE MAP OF THE INDIAN SUBCONTINENT

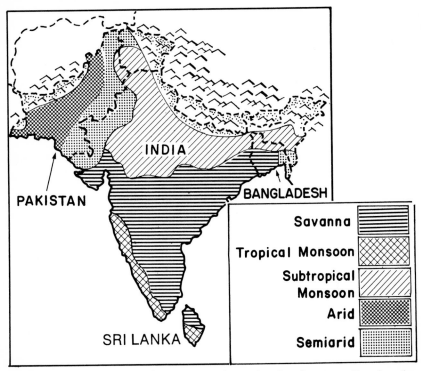

comfortable because there is no heat in the houses. In the dry season, no rain will fall for weeks at a time. In the wet season, there are heavy showers several times a day.

In the northern hill stations, temperatures sometimes fall below zero, while in the Ganges lowland and the Deccan plateau temperatures often reach 120°F. From December to March, the temperature on the coastal plains, washed by the warm waters of the Bay of Bengal and the Arabian Sea, is always between 70° and 90°. It is dry in most of the country, with warm days and cool nights.

The warm season begins in April; the hottest month is May. Dry weather continues, temperatures are high and dust storms are frequent. In the coastal areas the humidity is great because the air is heavy with the moisture that is being picked up from the nearby waters.

5

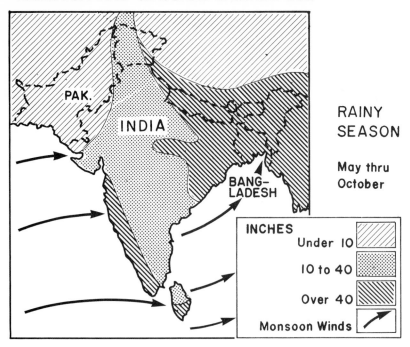

The rainy season follows the hot weather from June to September. Humidity is high, temperatures are a bit lower, and mildew is a constant problem.

The most comfortable months are October and November, after the rainy season is over. The sun shines and the temperatures rise.

The Monsoon. The very life of the people in this region depends upon the monoons. More than 80 percent of the annual rainfall is brought by the monsoons between June and September. If the monsoon winds do not arrive on time or bring sufficient rain, the land dries up and the food crop is poor, bringing famine and death to many, many people. If the rains come on time, and in large enough quantities, the fields are green, crops grow and there is food to feed the hundreds of millions of people.

MONSOON AND SEASONAL RAINFALL MAP

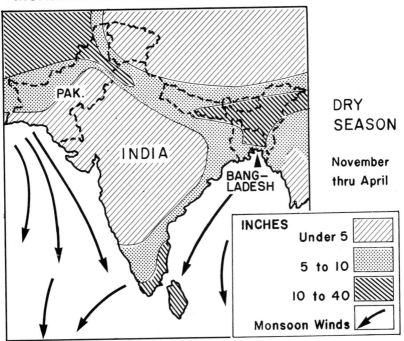

DRY
SEASON

November
thru April

INCHES
Under 5
5 to 10
10 to 40
Monsoon Winds

During the months of March, April and May, the sun heats the Indian subcontinent. The air above the land gets warm, and it rises like steam from a big oven. This low pressure area draws in warm, moist air from the Indian Ocean. From June to September the monsoon blows this moisture-laden air in a northeasterly direction over much of India. As the wind hits the Western Ghats, it begins to drop its moisture. Rain falls in great quantities along the coastal plains and western slopes of these mountains. The mountains, however, keep the Deccan plateau from getting more than a moderate rainfall.

The winds continue north of the Deccan and drop their rain south of the Himalayan Mountains. The Ganges valley receives nine-tenths of its annual 40-inch rainfall in a three-month period. (New York City also receives 40 inches of rain annually —from 2 to 4 inches a month throughout the whole year—but not 36 inches in a three-month period!)

7

Some places in India and Bangladesh get over 80 inches of rain. In Cherrapunji, a village in Assam in northeast India, the average rainfall is 450 inches a year! Raindrops as big as marbles fall during the monsoon season, and the villagers must protect themselves against their sting. On the other hand, Pakistan, and western and northwestern India are almost missed by the monsoon. They get eight or less inches of rain a year.

The coming of the summer monsoon is eagerly awaited by the people. One Indian author* described its arrival in the following way:

". . . There is a flash of lightning . . . the wind fills the black sails of the clouds. . . . A profound shadow falls on the earth. There is another clap of thunder. Big drops of rain fall and dry up in the dust. A fragrant smell rises from the earth. Another flash of lightning and another crack of thunder like the roar of a hungry tiger. It has come! Sheets of water, wave after wave. . . . All work stops . . .

"Once it is on, it stays for two months or more. . . . The earth becomes a big stretch of swamp and mud. Wells and lakes fill up and burst their bounds. In towns, gutters get clogged and streets become turbid streams. In villages, mud walls of huts melt in the water and thatched roofs sag and descend on the inmates. . . . Rivers . . . suddenly turn to floods. . . . Roads, railway tracks and bridges go under water. Houses near the riverbanks are swept down to the sea.

"With the monsoon, the tempo of life and death increases. Almost overnight grass begins to grow and leafless trees turn green. . . . Snakes, centipedes and scorpions are born out of nothing. . . . Inside rooms the hum of mosquitoes is maddening. While the monsoon lasts, the showers start and stop without warning. . . . Lightning and thunder never cease."

*From "Majra," by Khushwant Singh.

During the monsoon, the danger of floods is very real. Without the monsoon, however, there is no rain at all, or in such small amounts as to create very serious food problems.

Since ancient times, dams, canals and reservoirs have been built to store the water when there is too much, so it can be released when there is not enough rain. India has more land under irrigation than any other country in the world. Yet, with over 350 million acres under cultivation, much more of India's farmland must be freed from dependence on rainfall if it is to support the population.

C. RIVERS

The Indian subcontinent has three major river systems: The Indus and its tributaries in the west, the Ganges and its tributaries in the central and eastern part, and the Brahmaputra system in Assam in the west.

Between peninsular India and the Himalaya Mountains lie the alluvial plains enriched by these three great rivers. They rise in the mountains and water the most productive and densely populated section of India.

The Indus.   The Indus River has been so important in the history of India that its name was given to the whole country— Industan (Hindustan). It rises in Tibet, is fed by the glaciers of the Himalayas, and flows southwest for 1900 miles into Pakistan.

Civilization developed in the valley of the Indus as early as 2500 B.C. The ruins of Mohenjo-Daro show the site of a great city with public buildings and two-story houses of brick, surrounded by a great wall.

The Ganges.   The Ganges also rises in the Himalayas and flows for 1560 miles through the flat fields of Bengal where it meets the Brahmaputra in Bangladesh to form a vast delta along the Bay of Bengal. The second greatest river of India, the Jumna, joins the Ganges at Allahabad.

These river valleys are the most crowded sections of the

country. They are fertile and their waters are deep and broad enough for river transportation. On the Ganges' tributaries are found more of India's villages, more of its productive irrigated land, and more of its sprawling industries than anywhere else in India.

But the Ganges is more than just life-giving water. To the Hindus, the Ganges is sacred. They love the river because of its gifts to them. Hindus wish to be cremated on its banks and to have their ashes thrown into the river. They bathe in the river with faith that their sins, however bad, will be washed away and their souls will be purified. They call it "Ganga Mata," Mother Ganges.

The Brahmaputra.   The Brahmaputra rises in Tibet and, after spilling through the Himalayas, flows southwest and in Bangladesh bends south to join the tributaries of the Ganges. The river flows for nearly 700 miles through a region of tea plantations and rice fields in Assam. From there it flows south into the jute-growing sections of Bangladesh, and empties into the Bay of Bengal.

Other Rivers.   There are several other rivers in the Deccan region—the Narbada, Tapti, Godavari, Kistna and the Cauvery. The Narbada, Godavari and Cauvery are, like the Ganges, sacred rivers. Their banks are lined with Hindu temples and shrines. The Cauvery has been harnessed for irrigation and hydroelectric power. Other rivers dry up when there is little rainfall.

D.   PEOPLE AND LANGUAGES

A Mixture of Races.   From earliest times, people from other parts of the world have drifted into India and found new homes for themselves. They came as travellers, traders, or invaders. They settled down and were absorbed by the Indian population. At the same time they contributed their own patterns of culture and religion.

The earliest inhabitants of the Indus River Valley (2700 B.C.) were small, dark-skinned Dravidians. Then came the Aryans from central Asia about 2500 B.C. These Caucasian people were tall and light-skinned. Gradually, the Dravidians were pushed southward, and today they dominate the area from the Vindhya Mountains through the Deccan plateau to Cape Comorin. The northern part of India is inhabited mainly by the Indo-Aryan type. However, intermarriages between these two main groups and other racial groups have resulted in a fascinating mixture of human races.

A Variety of Languages.   India has not one, not two, but fifteen official languages, including Hindi and English. In addition 845 minor languages and dialects are spoken. Some of these dialects are related so that some of the people are able to understand each other fairly easily. Others are as different as Russian and English.

In general, India's languages come from two main language sources—Dravidian and Indo-Aryan. The Dravidian languages are spoken in the southern part of India. The Indo-Aryan languages, each of which has a different alphabet, are spoken in north and central India, and in Bangladesh and Pakistan. These languages, spoken by 75 per cent of the people of India, are of Sanskrit origin. Sanskrit is related to the Persian, Greek, Latin, Teutonic, Celtic and Slavic languages of Europe and the Middle East. Many English and European words are similar to Sanskrit words.

The Indian government has been faced with a serious problem in trying to secure a national language, namely the Hindi tongue. Riots in 1967 and 1968 broke out against this attempt. The government was forced to compromise and permit both English and Hindi.

Each of the Indian states has its own language. In 1966, the Sikhs created a new state and adopted Punjabi as the official language. All of these state languages, plus English, are recognized as official. However, communications between states or between a state and the national government must be made in English

India is a land whe
snake charmers entran
deadly cobras, villa
girls carry water jars
their heads, and far
ine is an ever-prese
danger.

MAJOR LANGUAGES OF INDIA

and in Hindi, the two official languages of the central government. English was given this special importance by the Indian constitution. In fact, several years ago, the Indian legislature decided to continue the use of English indefinitely.

Although only two per cent of the Indian people speak English today, it is the language of commerce, government and higher education. English is the one language that educated people from different parts of the country can use to understand each other.

Students in elementary schools learn their own regional language. In junior high school, Hindi is taught in areas where it is not usually spoken, then English is taught. In many school systems, Sanskrit is also required. Indian students may spend as much as half their time in the study of languages. Most

Indians, however, know only their regional language because the vast majority go only through the lower grades of elementary school.

The diversity of language has been condemned by some Indians as promoting disunity among the peoples of the subcontinent. They hope to see English eliminated, and Hindi made the one national language. This diversity has been favored by others, particularly government officials, because using the language of the people tends to promote democratic practices between ruler and ruled. Educated Indians favor English as a second language, so they can communicate with the rest of the world.

E. VILLAGES AND CITIES

More than 80 per cent of the people in this region are farmers and live in rural villages of 500 to 1000 people. The size of the some 600,000 villages varies according to the climate, location, and condition of the soil. The villages are the centers of local farming and social activities, as we shall learn later.

Many of these villages have none of the conveniences of modern living. Few of them have electricity, sewage systems or protected sources of water. Most villages have wells, and some, of course, are near rivers.

The villagers use small lanterns, candles, or kerosene, which is expensive. There is no local doctor. Most of India's doctors practice in the large cities. Sometimes there is a government nurse and a medical practitioner who is not a fully trained doctor. They use a small one- or two-room hospital or clinic to provide medical care for many villages.

The villagers are farmers, for the most part. Some, however, provide other services and goods for the entire community. There is a barber, a carpenter, sometimes a teacher. In return for their services to the farmers, they are paid in food. This exchange of goods for services, known as *jajmani*, involves very little cash. Traditionally, some families specialize in certain occupations which have been passed down over the centuries.

14

Many villages depend upon the life-giving water of a deep well, dug centuries ago.

The one-room houses are very simple; their walls and floor are made of mud, the roof of thatch. There are neither windows nor plumbing. The only furniture is a *charpoy*—a cot with a wooden frame and a lattice of ropes which serves as the spring, or a straw mat called a *chatai*. There are no chairs or tables.

Cooking utensils are made of wood or pottery, sometimes of brass. Because of the mild weather, cooking is done and meals are eaten outdoors; everyone squats on his heels and uses his right hand to eat. In Bangladesh they eat rice; in the Punjab they eat a pancake made of wheat called *chappatti*. Sometimes mangoes, dates and bananas are part of the meal if they are raised in the neighborhood.

Since it is against the Hindu religion to eat beef, eggs and fish are sometimes eaten. Indians eat vegetables such as eggplant, peppers, tomatoes, potatoes and beans. In most parts of the region, the staples are rice, milk, *ghee* (liquid butter), and yogurt. Alcohol is forbidden by religion and by law in most of India.

The urban population in India is rapidly approaching 100 million. Crowding and lack of adequate housing and health care creates severe problems.

15

India has eighteen major cities, each of which has a population of over 500,000.

Delhi. Delhi and New Delhi are twin cities located on the Jumna River in northwest India. Their combined population is over 3½ million. Delhi's old city wall, narrow streets, bazaars and exquisite handicrafts show Oriental influence.

New Delhi, the capital of India, has broad boulevards, wide avenues, gardens, beautiful lawns, pools, modern office buildings, fashionable shops, a racetrack, two golf courses and two airports. These cities are the leading trade centers of northwest India, as well as the center of political life.

However, there are also "rooms" not fit for one person which are occupied by six, as in the Harijan Colony. Traffic is heavy. There are a great number of pedestrians and bicyclists. Beggars and holy men are everywhere.

In Bombay, luxury towers overshadow impoverished shacks of the poor.

United Nations/J. P. Laffonte

Calcutta. This city, with its sprawling industrial and residential suburbs, is the largest Indian city. There are over 8.3 million inhabitants, some packed into flimsy, one-room huts. Many of the homeless people sleep on the sidewalks. Calcutta is in the center of India's most highly developed commercial and industrial area, and is a major seaport.

Bombay. Bombay, a very large city, has a population of over 7.6 million. This busy city has the bustling atmosphere of a large Western city with its skyscrapers and big office buildings. Its harbor on the Arabian Sea is the best in the country. Through it flows most of India's imports and exports.

Madras. This big city of about 2 million residents is the main trade port for south India. Madras is a center of the fine arts, music and dance. Its many Hindu temples were built during a great period of religious art between A.D. 600 and 1600.

Hyderabad. Located on the Deccan plateau, this city of about 1.3 million people is the main city of central India. Muslim rule for centuries has given it a distinctly Muslim appearance with its many mosques and minarets.

Other cities in India that have a population of almost one million include Bangalore, Kanpur, and Ahmadabad. There are several important religious centers, including Benares, the most famous holy city of the Hindus on the Ganges River, and Madurai.

F.   AGRICULTURE AND MINERALS

Farming is the major occupation in all three countries of the Indian subcontinent. Three-quarters of the people depend on cultivation of the land for their livelihood. The variety of climate, the abundance of rain, the many irrigation projects to store water, and the immense number of hungry people to feed are all factors that explain the importance of farming to the people in the region.

The production of food crops exceeds that of non-food crops. Among the leading products grown in this region are:

1. Rice. About a third of India's farmlands are devoted to the raising of rice—India's most important crop. Rice is raised in the coastal areas of the peninsula in the south, in the lower Ganges plain and in Assam where rainfall is very heavy. Although India produces 25 per cent of the world's rice, it is not enough for its people's needs. Great quantities of rice must be imported from Burma and the United States.

2. Wheat and Other Grains. Wheat, India's second most important cereal grain, is raised in the drier interior and in the northwest. Although India raises more than 90 million tons a year, wheat must also be imported—most of it from the United States and Canada. Barley, millet, and corn are also grown in large quantities.

3. Tea. The chief producing areas are along the slopes of the Himalaya and Ghat Mountains, and in northern Bangladesh. India produces 40 per cent of the world's tea, and exports most of it.

4. Sugar Cane. India is fourth among the nations of the world in the production of sugar cane. It is raised in the irrigated lands of the upper Indus River and in the foothills of the Himalayas.

5. Cotton. The chief cotton-growing region is in the Deccan. India is among the largest cotton-producing countries in the world. Indian cotton has short fibers because, during the growing season, the Deccan region does not get enough rain so the cotton is picked before it grows long. The cotton cloth made from short-fiber cotton is not as fine as American cotton cloth, but it is widely used throughout India and other Asiatic countries.

6. Jute. This plant is raised particularly in the northeast province of Bengal, much of which is now Bangladesh. The fertile soil, heavy rainfall, abundant sunshine and the large number of available workers have helped to make this an important crop. From this plant comes a coarse fiber which is made into burlap bags, rope, twine and carpets. Much American cotton is wrapped in burlap made in the subcontinent. Burlap is a leading export of India because, though the jute is raised in Bangladesh, the cloth is made in India.

India also raises peanuts which are used for cattle feed and the manufacture of peanut oil. Most of the world's shellac is supplied by India. This product comes from a substance deposited by insects on trees. Coffee, nuts and spices (cinnamon, ginger, pepper) are grown along the Malabar coast.

India has more cattle than any other country in the world. These animals are protected because cows provide the main source of milk, and bulls are used as work animals on the farms. However, the skins of the animals are made into leather—a major export.

India and Bangladesh have much land that is fit for cultivation, and produce large food crops, but the ever-increasing populations of these countries raise very serious food problems. Many families have very tiny farms of one or two acres and can barely grow enough food to feed themselves. Most of the milk, vegetables, fruit and grain grown on the farm is used on the farm.

Poor, even primitive farming methods also help to keep food production down. The yields per acre of farmland are among the lowest in the world. For example, India raises 13.3 bushels of wheat per acre, compared to the American average of 27.2 bushels per acre. India's production of rice—1438 pounds per acre—may be compared to Japanese production of 4300 pounds and U.S. production of 4250 pounds per acre.

Farm tools are very inefficient. Seeds are not carefully chosen

CASE INQUIRY: Youth in India

The following excerpts illustrate the various activities, interests, and goals of youth in India. The first section deals with youngsters who received awards for bravery; the second section looks at young women and their roles in Indian society.

> The youngest of the group, nine-year-old Nabin Chandra Ghosh, hailing from West Bengal, snatched away a gun from the dacoits [robbers] who raided his house in a miraculous feat, killed the ring leader and injured others, thus saving his father's life.
>
> Master Bhagirath Singh, twelve, from Jharia in Bihar, shot and killed a big hyena who had become a menace to the villagers.
>
> Kumaran P. Raju from Alleppy (Kerala) pushed to safety a six-year-old student drowning in the river.
>
> A similar feat was performed by Rajan Pandurang Patil from Bombay, who rescued four out of thirteen children who fell in a well following an accident.
>
> * * *
>
> A familiar face at flower exhibitions in New Delhi is that of pretty Neelam Badlani, a "flower girl" in her early twenties.
>
> Neelam has a way with flowers, she has bagged as many as eight prizes for her flower arrangements. She is especially proud of the special cash award by the Health Ministry for her rose exhibit entitled, "Hum Do Hamara Do" ["We are two, ours are two"] a rather original and novel idea to promote family planning.
>
> Working as a receptionist at the Indian Standards Institution, Neelam is also keenly interested in designing her clothes and in movies.
>
> Eighteen-year-old Rani Verma, rather surprisingly, has unorthodox views on most subjects. This can perhaps be attributed to her fondness for reading and for writing, especially short stories and plays.
>
> Currently studying for the B.A. examination, Rani is keen on sitting for the Indian Administrative Service examination. She is critical of the system of education in [India]. . . and realizes that unless educational reforms are effected immediately there is little hope for our students in the face of world competition.

1. What can you infer about village life in India from the section on youngesters who received awards?

2. What do the activities and views of the young Indian women suggest in terms of social change and women's roles in India?

Voices from India edited by Margaret Cormack and Kiki Skagen. Praeger Publishers, New York, 1972, pages 236–238.

and poor seed is mixed with richer types, resulting in poor yields. The lack of fertilizer to restore the tired soil is also a reason for the poor yield of Indian farmers. Because it is a crime to cut down trees to use for fuel, farmers burn cow dung for fuel instead of using it for fertilizer.

India does not raise enough food for its people. When the monsoon does not provide the water necessary to raise crops, the Indian people are faced with hunger and famine. In 1965 and 1966, when the monsoon rains failed, thousands would have died if the United States and other nations had not sent in millions of tons of wheat. From 1967-72, sufficient rain, combined with scientific farming and irrigation techniques, increased rice and wheat production. The drought and food shortages returned in 1972-75. Since 1976 rain and even flooding has returned.

Minerals.   This region has large supplies of some of the most important minerals needed by the world today. India's rich mineral reserves make it a leading producer of iron ore. India mines about 70 million tons of coal a year. Almost all of it goes to the railroads and to the steel plants; little is exported or used for fuel. India ranks third in the mining of manganese, which is used in making steel. The Tata steel plant at Jamshedpur, in the northeast, is the largest in India; it produces almost one million tons a year. India ranks as the third largest steel-producing country in Asia, after Japan and Communist China.

India has a rich supply of other useful minerals such as ilmenite (for titanium), bauxite (to make aluminum), monazite from which uranium and thorium are derived, and talc. It is the world's largest supplier of mica. Its gold mines are among the richest in the world. Diamonds, sapphires and emeralds are also mined.

Although some petroleum has been found in India, it is far from enough for the country's needs, and additional supplies have to be imported. India lacks important minerals such as lead, zinc, copper, tin and nickel which are needed in modern industries. Future exploration of the country may uncover other natural resources that may be of use to the Indians.

21

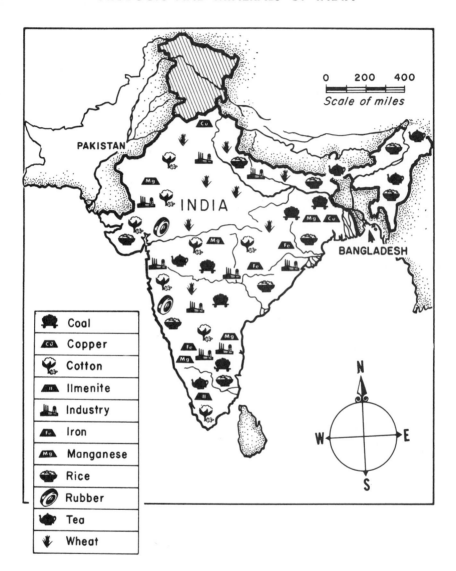

Forests. Forests cover 150 million square miles of India—about one-fifth of the land. On the lower slopes of the Himalayas there are fir, spruce, cedar, deodar and blue pine trees. Below this area of cone-bearing trees, forests of oak, chestnut and walnut can be found. There are forests of exotic woods such as sandalwood, satinwood, teak, acacia, and ebony, used for decorative objects. The timber is used for building purposes, and for making charcoal, paper, matches and plywood.

The number of mills for processing wood products is growing. In addition, the forests yield large supplies of resins, gums, essential oils, and tanning materials.

Animals. Although Hindus do not eat beef, there are over 200 million cattle and buffaloes in India. They are used as work animals and for their milk. The 40 million sheep produce quantities of wool.

There are monkeys, baboons, deer, wild boar, elephants, tigers, leopards, crocodiles and alligators. Elephants are trained to do many heavy tasks. The various "cats" are a constant danger to jungle villagers. There are also deadly snakes such as the cobra.

Water Power. Although India is potentially rich in water power because of its many rivers, the amount of electricity produced from water power is small in comparison to its needs. Electricity is used for many of the large factories, but very few villages have electric light.

India's potential for hydroelectric power is one of the highest in the world, but little of it has been developed. Large dams for irrigation, flood control and electric power have been built, and miles of transmission lines have been laid. Yet India produces only about 50 million kilowatt hours of electricity per year, compared with over one billion kilowatt hours per year for the United States. India and Pakistan are hoping to develop the use of nuclear power to supply electricity cheaply.

Transportation. India has the largest railroad system in Asia —the fourth largest in the world. There are over 35,000 miles of track. The railroads carry most of the freight and a large part of the passenger traffic, but there still are not enough trains. The efficiency of the railroads is further complicated by the use of four different gauges (track widths).

In a remote village, a man weaves fibers into mats and baskets. Such cottage industry is common throughout India.

Automobiles and trucks are becoming more common, but the high cost of scarce gasoline limits their usefulness. There are over 530,000 miles of roads; only about 160,000 miles are hard-surfaced or concrete, the rest are dirt. Most local transportation is by oxcart, bicycle, or by foot.

India has 74 civil airports, local and international. Air-India offers overseas service and the flight by jet from New York to Bombay takes less than 17 hours. (It took Vasco da Gama over 11 months to sail from Portugal to Calicut in 1498!)

Water transportation is important in coastal areas and on parts of the Ganges and Brahmaputra rivers in northeast India and Bangladesh. Many of the rivers cannot be depended upon because they dry up during the hot months preceding the arrival of the monsoon. Also the large amounts of water removed from the rivers for irrigation purposes further reduces the water level of these rivers.

Manufacturing. Cottage industries, that is, goods produced in the home, account for the largest part of manufactured merchandise and the largest number of workers. These home workshops hand loom cotton, silk and wool, and process most agricultural products. Highly skilled artisans work in brass, copper, silver, gold and exotic woods to make artistic objects for export.

Textile manufacturing is the largest industry that uses power-driven machines. India and Bangladesh have contributed to the fashion world such well-known materials as calico, muslin, cashmere and madras. Large mills turn out fabrics made of cotton and jute. Other plants produce cigarettes, sugar, vegetable oils and articles made of rubber or leather.

Heavy industry includes steel mills, aluminum and cement factories, chemical, fertilizer and machine tool plants.

QUESTIONS AND ACTIVITIES

MULTIPLE CHOICE TEST

In each of the following, you have three choices. Choose the only correct answer.

1. The main idea of this chapter is to describe (*a*) the history of India, (*b*) Muslim rule in India, (*c*) the physical features of the Indian subcontinent.
2. India is (*a*) the largest country in Asia, (*b*) smaller than the United States,(*c*) as big as South America.

3. India's population is (*a*) exceeded only by Communist China, (*b*) as large as the United States, (*c*) greater than Communist China.
4. The most important mountain chain in the Indian subcontinent is (*a*) the Alps, (*b*) the Himalayas, (*c*) the Ghats.
5. India's main rivers (*a*) originate in the Himalaya Mountains, (*b*) empty into the Bay of Bengal, (*c*) flow in a north-south direction.
6. The winds that bring rain to this region's farms are the (*a*) easterlies, (*b*) monsoons, (*c*) hurricanes.
7. The Malabar coast on the western side of India is (*a*) a desert area, (*b*) a rich agricultural center, (*c*) a large industrial region.
8. The heavy rain season in India and Bangladesh occurs during the months of (*a*) February to April, (*b*) April to June, (*c*) June to September.
9. The longest river in India is the (*a*) Ganges, (*b*) Indus, (*c*) Brahmaputra.
10. The largest city in India is (*a*) Calcutta, (*b*) Delhi, (*c*) Bombay.
11. Most of the people of India live in (*a*) small villages, (*b*) large cities, (*c*) medium-sized towns.
12. The Aryans were (*a*) Asiatic tribesmen who wandered into India, (*b*) the original inhabitants of India, (*c*) foreign invaders from the northwest.
13. The languages spoken by most of the Indian people are derived from the (*a*) Sanskrit, (*b*) Tamil, (*c*) Hungarian.
14. The common language spoken by educated people from different parts of India is (*a*) Hindi, (*b*) English, (*c*) Punjabi.
15. The language spoken by more people in India than any other language is (*a*) Hindi, (*b*) English, (*c*) Tamil.
16. Each of the 22 states in India has (*a*) a different system of government, (*b*) its own official language, (*c*) its own form of education.
17. India's most important food crop is (*a*) corn, (*b*) rice, (*c*) wheat.
18. To raise rice, (*a*) a lot of water is needed, (*b*) much machinery is necessary, (*c*) a dry climate is essential.
19. Most of the tea raised in India is (*a*) used by the people, (*b*) exported, (*c*) converted into cattle feed.
20. India supplies most of the world's (*a*) leather goods, (*b*) peanuts, (*c*) shellac.

21. India (*a*) raises enough food to feed its own people, (*b*) must import rice, even though it raises one-quarter of the world's supply, (*c*) exports large quantities of foodstuffs to its neighbors.
22. Jute is used (*a*) to make burlap bags, (*b*) for seats and cushions in American cars, (*c*) for building purposes.
23. Indian farming methods (*a*) help make the country self-sufficient in food, (*b*) are among the most advanced in the world, (*c*) limit the productivity of the farmlands.
24. Most of the coal mined in India is used (*a*) to make steel, (*b*) for fuel, (*c*) as an export to other countries.
25. India's railroad system (*a*) is the largest in Asia, (*b*) is adequate for its transportation needs, (*c*) is highly modernized.

KEY WORDS AND PHRASES

Can you explain the meaning of the following words or phrases? Refer to your dictionary if necessary.

monsoon   "bread basket of India"
Sanskrit   Aryan
Indo-European   subcontinent
alluvium   jute
Dravidian   ghee

INTERPRETATION QUESTIONS

Answer the following questions. Refer, if necessary, to the maps in this chapter.

1. How does the Indian subcontinent compare in size to the United States?
2. Which country is most crowded, the United States, India or Bangladesh?
3. How does the topography of northern India differ from that of southern India?
4. Most of the rivers of India flow in an east-west direction. Why?
5. Is the Indian subcontinent on, below, or above the equator?
6. What is the great river of northern India?
7. What nations are neighbors of India, on the east; on the west?
8. In what country do the Ganges and Brahmaputra rivers meet and empty into the Bay of Bengal?

TRUE OR FALSE

Do you agree or disagree with the following statements? Give reasons for your answers.

1. The Ganges is the most sacred river of the Hindus.
2. The capital of India is New Delhi.
3. The Indian subcontinent has the same climate in the north and in the south.
4. The monsoon is the most important factor in the life of the Indian farmer.
5. Rainfall is heavy on the Deccan plateau.
6. English is spoken by only 2 per cent of the Indian people yet is one of the most important languages in India today.
7. Farming methods in this region are very primitive.
8. India is self-sufficient in important mineral resources.
9. The chief export crop of Bangladesh is jute.
10. Most, but not all, of the Indian people belong to the Caucasian race.

THINGS TO DO

1. Have students prepare a five-minute talk on each of the following topics:
   a. The conquest of Mt. Everest.
   b. The Monsoons—Curse or Blessing?
   c. Sanskrit—the mother tongue of many languages.
   d. The steel industry of India.
2. Prepare a series of charts to show the percentages of India's production in relation to the rest of the world in the following products: cotton, rice, wheat, jute, steel. (Use an almanac to find this information).
3. Develop a bulletin board display of pictures about "The peoples and languages of the Indian subcontinent."
4. Draw a map of the region showing the important rivers, mountains, bodies of water, chief cities, natural resources and language groups.
5. Prepare a class debate on the topic: "India has the potential to become a great nation."
6. Plan a two-week vacation to either India, Pakistan, or Bangladesh. How will you travel within the country? What cities will you visit. What types of food will you eat? See your local travel agent or the tourist board of the country for information.

THE RELIGIONS OF INDIA

2

A. HINDUISM

The largest single religion of the many religions in India is Hinduism. About 520 million Indians, by far the majority of the people, call themselves Hindus.

To many of these people, Hinduism is more than a religion. It is a way of life. It provides a rule for everything they do or may do from the moment of birth to the moment of death. It tells them when to wash and how to wash, what to eat and how to eat it, what clothes to wear and when to wear them, how to greet people and how to say goodbye.

Hinduism is also a social system. Its many castes and sub-castes divide people into groups according to birth and occupation. With these divisions come rules and regulations concerning social relations between members of the same caste, and between those of different castes.

Hinduism is a philosophy. It explains the moral obligations of man and his duties in his various roles of husband, father, family provider and ruler.

Unlike other great religions, Hinduism has no one founder (like Jesus or Mohammed), no central authority (like the Catholic Pope), no organization (like the Catholic Church), no main religious book (like the Bible or the Koran), and no fixed creed.

Hindus have a variety of beliefs and practices. Some believe that God is everywhere—in every rock, every tree, every particle of matter—and because people are different they need different ways of approaching God. They believe in a Supreme Being who is called Brahma. But Brahma takes many forms and has different functions. This has led to the worship of various deities, many of whom are local or village gods.

Devout Hindus bathe in the Ganges, most sacred of rivers, to wash away sin and evil.

In addition to Brahma, the creator, other important gods are Vishnu, the preserver, and Siva, the destroyer (of ignorance and evil). Because Hinduism is a tolerant religion, accepting all other beliefs and adding new beliefs to its ancient ones, it is difficult for other religions to gain a foothold in India.

If Hinduism does not have a Bible or a Koran, where then may one find its religious beliefs and practices written down?

Sources of Hinduism. Hinduism is one of the oldest faiths among the great religions of the world. Its basic ideas were brought into northwest India by the Aryan invaders in 1500 B.C. and written down in Sanskrit. The scriptures venerated by all Hindus are the *Vedas,* or collections of sacred psalms, prayers, magic charms, and chants. The *Vedas* tell of nature worship. There were gods of the sun, the wind and the rain. The most famous *veda* was the *Rig-Veda,* the oldest religious document in history (800 B.C.).

In the *Rig-Veda* is found a "Hymn of Creation" in which a universal spirit is mentioned. Part of it is as follows:

30

"Darkness was hidden in a deeper darkness;
This All was as a sea without dimensions,
The void still held unformed what was potential,
Until the power of Warmth produced the sole One . . .
Whether he made the world or did not make it,
He knows whence this creation came, he only
Who in the highest heaven guards and watches;
He knows indeed, but then, perhaps he knows not!"

Read these lines out loud. Ask yourself the meaning of the third and fourth lines. How does the fifth line remind you of the first book of the Old Testament? And what does the last line mean to you?

Another source of information about Hinduism is the *Brahmanas*. These are collections of rituals and ceremonies, composed in the 8th and 7th centuries B.C. The *Upanishads* are commentaries on the individual soul and the origin of the universe. They were written about 600 B.C. Then there is the *Law Book of Manu* (250 B.C.) which regulates social and daily life in terms of religion.

Great Stories.   Great epic masterpieces tell us much about folk Hinduism. The two most important are the *Mahabharata*, the longest poem ever written, and the *Ramayana*.

1. The *Mahabharata* was written several centuries before Christ, and has had a great influence on Hindu character and conduct. The most famous section of the long poem is the *Bhagavad-Gita* (A.D. 1) which deals with the correctness of warfare and suggests the possibility of universal salvation.

It tells the story of Arjuna, the perfect warrior, on the eve of an important battle between rival armies. Arjuna was unhappy because in the army opposing him were many of his friends and relatives. He did not want to kill them, but he didn't want to lose the fight either.

He turned for advice to his charioteer who revealed himself as Krishna, one of the gods. Krishna explained to the warrior that the purpose of life is to know God. This can be accomplished by meditation, by good conduct in this world and by loving devotion. God may be reached by man's efforts which will lead him to truth and salvation. Krishna also spoke to Arjuna about the duties of all the people, the organization of society, the obligation of each man to do his duty, and the good results that are brought by good deeds. The story ends with Arjuna victorious in the battle.

The high moral tone of Krishna's advice has had a profound influence on Hindus throughout the centuries. Gandhi, of whom we shall learn much more later in this book, called the *Bhagavad-Gita* a "dictionary of conduct," from which he drew the inspiration for his doctrine of non-violence.

2. The *Ramayana* tells the story of the god Rama and his wife Sita. Rama lost his throne because his father, King Dasratha, kept a promise made to his queen whereby the throne would go to Rama's stepbrother. For years Rama and Sita travelled throughout India and had many adventures.

One day Sita was kidnapped by the evil king Ravana of Ceylon. She was finally rescued by brave Rama, his loyal brother Lakshamana, and the daring Hanuman, the monkey general and his monkey army. Hanuman set Ravana's palace on fire by lighting his own tail and swinging from one part of the palace to another. (It is because of the great help of the monkey army in this story that monkeys are considered sacred by the Hindus.)

After a long exile, Rama returned to his kingdom to assume his rightful place on the throne. Whether Sita returned with him to rule as his queen is not clear. One account tells how they lived happily together for many years as rulers of the kingdom. Another version tells that Rama was forced to send Sita away because his people thought she had been unfaithful to him while in captivity.

To generations of Hindus, Rama and Sita have shown how human beings should behave. The loyalty, love, devotion, obedience and sense of duty in this often-repeated story have been an inspiration to Hindu children.

32

Chief Religious Ideas. Three main concepts in Hinduism provide unifying elements in a religion that tolerates so many differences in social structure and the worship of so many gods.

1. Reincarnation. The Hindu religion teaches that a person's soul never dies, only his body does. Upon death, the soul moves into the body of another living thing—a person or an animal. This belief in the transmigration of souls is called *samsara*. The soul is reborn in another body, then goes again through death and rebirth in an effort to achieve *moksha*—the final state of salvation and freedom from the life-death cycle.

Living things are not all equal according to this teaching. A crawling insect, a four-legged animal, a bird, a man—all are different rungs on the ladder reaching toward *moksha*. A soul moves up or down on this ladder according to its *karma*.

2. Karma. This is the belief that a person's actions in life determine his future state in his next rebirth. Good behavior will bring promotion to a higher level; bad behavior will bring demotion to a lower level—to a lower caste or perhaps even to that of an insect.

The word *karma* means "deed." A person's present state is the result of all his previous acts; his present and future acts determine his future state. A person cannot escape the result of his actions. If a person or an animal lives a good life, and does what he is supposed to do, his soul will be rewarded by being reincarnated in the next rebirth into a higher-ranking human or animal. Good behavior and a good life are determined by *dharma*.

3. Dharma. This is the set of rules that must be followed by each living thing if it desires to be promoted in its next reincarnation. This "path of righteousness" is different for each living thing. A person's *dharma* includes his obligations and duties within the family and the society into which he was born. "It is better to do one's own *dharma* poorly than to do another's well" is an ancient Indian proverb. The Hindu, therefore, is offered the hope that he may determine his future in the next life by his actions in his present life.

33

Religious Practices. The Hindus follow strict rituals of washing and cleanliness, faithful worship at shrines, and severe dietary laws.

1. Hindus from all over India spend months making pilgrimages on foot to holy cities like Benares.

2. Hindus wash their hands and feet in pools before praying daily at the many temples. They bathe in sacred rivers like the Ganges, the most sacred of them all, to wash away sin and evil.

3. When a person dies he or she is cremated the same day. A male is wrapped in white cloth, a female in red cloth. The eldest son walks around the pyre three times and prays before starting the fire. In the past, the dead man's wife would throw herself into the flames and join him after death *(suttee)*. This practice has been outlawed by the government, although the change met much resistance. The Burning Ghats of most cities are holy places.

4. The Hindus consider the cow sacred, and it may not be slaughtered. India has more cattle than any other country in the world even though hunger and starvation face the people very often. Because of their feeling that cows are sacred, most Hindus are vegetarians; they will not eat meat. Some cattle are used for plowing, the cows for milking. Many others belong to no one and roam the streets of villages, even of cities, and go unharmed.

The Caste System. The caste system has been so closely related to Indian life for the past 3000 years that it is difficult to consider it as separate from religious life.

The caste system was introduced by the Aryan tribes who invaded India about 1500 B.C. These conquering Aryans forced the conquered Dravidians to become their servants and perform the work needed to maintain society. Thus, the caste system originated as social and economic distinctions.

By the caste system all people were divided into groups according to birth and hereditary occupation. There were five main castes and over 3000 sub-castes. The main castes were:

1. The Brahmans, or priestly class and cultured élite

CASE INQUIRY: Caste in the Villages

The following selection is taken from a book written by an Indian woman journalist some fifteen years after Indian independence and a dozen years after untouchability had been abolished.

> In the same village I walked into the house of a grey-bearded Sikh peasant. Though not too impressive or clean, his house is big. In the courtyard two beautiful big bullocks are standing with a bright yellow cloth covering their backs. Cotton is lying on the ground to dry. The man has sufficient land, and according to him everything is fine. He is not a refugee and his fortunes therefore have not suffered any recent upheaval. Just then a woman comes in, wearing a blue *salwar* and *kameez* (baggy trousers and a long skirt). A warm shawl covers her head and part of the face. Slim, light of skin and with buck teeth and dirty hands she is obviously very angry. Mistaking me perhaps for an emissary of the government, she lets forth a torrent of complaints: not only is the present administration not doing anything for the *zemindars* [landlords], but it is positively conspiring against them.
>
> "But why are you so angry?" I ask mildly as soon as I can get in a word.
>
> "Why?" she repeats. "The government has given land to *Harijans* [Untouchables] in this village. The result is that they will not do our work. And now I, a *Jat* woman" (with heavy emphasis on the word *Jat*) "I have to dirty my hands and do this work of making cowdung cakes. Is this a *Jat's* work?"
>
> "But don't you want the condition of *Harijans* also to improve?" I ask.
>
> "Why should it?" is the forceful reply with the full weight of conviction behind it. *"Harijans* were born to do menial jobs. God made them such, and they should be allowed to continue as such. Am I meant for this—do I deserve it?" and she holds out her dirty hands to invite sympathy.

1. In this section of India, the Jats are comfortably well off, although they are members of a peasant caste. Why would these people feel threatened by the improvement in Untouchables' lives?

2. What methods can a country use to make such change more acceptable to its people?

Blossoms in the Dust by Kusum Nair. Praeger Publishers, Inc., New York, 1961, pages 109–110.

2. The Kshatriyas, or warrior class, and ruling aristocracy
3. The Vaisyas, or farmer, professional and artisan class
4. The Shudras, or menial, servant class
5. The Untouchables, or lowest class, called variously "out-casts," "scheduled class," and by Gandhi "children of God," or *harijan.*

A man who was born into his caste remained in that caste for the rest of his life. Born a street cleaner's son, he must be a street cleaner; born a merchant's son, he must be a merchant. Perhaps in a later life, if he followed his *dharma* conscientiously and well, he might become something better.

A person could marry only within his own caste. He could have social relations only with people belonging to his caste. Each caste had its own code of behavior, duties and responsibilities. This code influenced the education, occupation, diet, marriage, and social privileges of every member in the caste.

Under the caste system, everyone knew what was expected of him. The tailor, the carpenter, the blacksmith, the farmer, the teacher—each had his life laid out for him. If he were dissatisfied with his rank in life, he could hope that in his next reincarnation his soul would be promoted to a higher sub-caste, or even to a higher caste.

The Untouchables. Although listed as the lowest of the castes, they were considered "outcasts"—they did not belong. Over 40 million Untouchables were considered unfit to worship in Hindu temples, were prohibited from using public roads, could not let their children play with the children of any other caste. They were limited to the lowest occupations such as street cleaners or tanners. Since the skin of a sacred cow cannot be handled by a caste Hindu, this job was left to the non-caste people.

The lot of the millions of Untouchables has improved considerably in the last twenty-five years. Gandhi began a campaign to raise their status and accepted them as his pupils. The Indian constitution (1950) abolished untouchability, and made discrimination against any citizen on the grounds of religion, race, caste, sex or place of birth punishable by law. In 1968 a new law provided that 12.5 per cent of government jobs were to go to ex-Untouchables, now officially called "Scheduled Castes." Many Scheduled Caste members have entered politics, and throughout India *harijans* have come to active political leadership. Yet even in politics, where the votes of the Scheduled Castes are heavy, great discrimination remains.

Weakening Caste Lines. Today the caste system is still practiced in India, although the origins of the system are hidden in antiquity. Custom and tradition change slowly although many factors are weakening the system. These include:

1. The great increase in educational opportunities for more and more Indians, regardless of past status, and the improvement of status due to the availability of better jobs.

2. The increasing movement of people from villages to cities with large populations where caste lines are blurred, castes mingle and caste restrictions have less importance.

3. The constitutional changes favoring Untouchables, and also the universal suffrage law which gives all people, male and female regardless of caste membership, equal right to vote.

4. Leadership of people like Gandhi, who fought discrimination, and of Indira Gandhi (no relation) who was the first woman to become Indian Prime Minister.

5. The growth of industry, with increasing need for jobs that cut across caste lines.

Continuing Caste Strength. The caste system has not, however, completely disappeared from India. It will take many, many years before all traces of it vanish. Caste is still very strong in the villages, and most of the people of India live in villages. There, change is very slow. The influences of education and industrialization have only begun to be felt in villages.

For example, caste is still the most important consideration when marriage is being planned. Many Indians consider the caste system an essential part of Hinduism, and they cannot separate their religious beliefs from the social practices of caste. Thus, a Hindu's acceptance of the religious doctrines of *karma* and *dharma* includes the obligations of caste membership. India is slow to change, and nowhere as slow as in its attitude toward caste.

B.   OTHER RELIGIONS IN INDIA

Islam.   The second great religion in India, after Hinduism, is Islam, with about 60 million followers who call themselves Muslims. Islam is the religious faith preached by the Arab prophet Muhammad who lived during the 7th century A.D. After his death in 632, the religion spread rapidly along the shores of North Africa, into Spain and Portugal, and across the Asiatic mainland. It first came into India in the 8th century; then there was a second and greater wave in the 13th century.

Islam, an Arabic word, means both submission to God, and peace. Muslims and Hindus are very different in their beliefs and practices. The Muslims worship one God, Allah; the Hindus have many gods. The Muslims have their holy book, the *Koran*; the Hindus have no such book. The Muslims do not allow any images of living things in their religion; the Hindus have many. The Muslims are meat-eaters, though they must not eat pork; the Hindus are vegetarians.

The Muslims have a few very important religious practices. They must recite prayers five times a day facing Mecca, the holy city where Muhammad was born. Once in a lifetime, if possible, Muslims must make a pilgrimage to Mecca. They must fast from early morning to sunset for a month. They must remove their shoes at the door of a mosque, and wash before prayer. They must not fight, gamble, or drink alcohol. They must help orphans and be generous to the poor, and kind to strangers. The Hindus have many more practices, as we have learned, no two of which are universal among all Hindus.

Jainism.   As early as the 6th century B.C. some Hindus revolted against some of the early Hindu practices. The cult of animal sacrifices in which the Brahmans, the priests, were so important, was particularly distasteful. They exalted reflection and meditation above these rituals.

In Magadha (Bihar), after twelve years of reflection, a religious teacher who was called Mahavira ("great hero") and Jaina ("victor") proclaimed himself the prophet of a new religion which still has about 2 million members today.

The Jainists vow to kill no living thing, tell no lies and steal nothing. They carry their most important religious belief, non-violence toward all living things (*ahimsa*), to extremes sometimes. Monks and nuns of the Jainist order go around completely veiled so they will not, even by accident, swallow an insect. They carry small brooms to sweep ahead of their feet so they won't step on bugs.

Lay members of this religion live in the large cities of western India, are usually merchants, and often very wealthy. They believe strongly in education, and are very strict vegetarians. Although relatively few in number, they have had considerable influence upon other Indians.

Buddhism.   One of the great religions of the world, Buddhism, developed in India in the 6th and 5th centuries B.C. It spread throughout the subcontinent, then moved across frontiers to other Asian countries. It has nearly disappeared in India, however, the land of its origin. There are only about 4.3 million Buddhists in India today.

The founder of this religion was Siddhartha Gautama (563-487 B.C.), born of royal family in a small kingdom at the foothills of the Himalayan Mountains. His father surrounded him with every luxury and shielded him from all unpleasant things. His life was changed when he was about thirty years old. One day, while riding outside the palace, he saw a bent, tired old man for the first time in his life. He was shocked to realize that all men become old. When he saw crippled, diseased and dead people, he realized that life was not all pleasure.

The religion and philosophy of Hinduism continues to have a tremendous effect upon life in India today. Many beautiful pieces of art, statuary, and shrines have been built to honor the Hindu gods.

Mathura Museum

The Metropolitan Museum of Art, Eggleston Fund, 1927

The statue of Brahma (above) dates back to the tenth century. Another important god in the Hindu religion is Vishnu, the preserver (left).

These sights troubled him and set him thinking about the meaning of life.

He left his beautiful wife and new-born son and wandered for six years throughout the country, seeking answers to his questions about the behavior of people and the meaning of life from the great thinkers of the time. The answers came to him suddenly, as an inspiration, and made him the "Enlightened One" or Buddha.

Buddha spent forty years in teaching his beliefs. The secret of life's meaning was to be found in the *Four Noble Truths*: (1) Life is full of pain and suffering. (2) Man's desires cause this suffering. (3) By putting an end to desire, man can end suffering. (4) There is a way to end desire. In other words, desire for things, not the lack of the possessions themselves, was the root of unhappiness.

The way to eliminate desire was through the *Eightfold Path*: (1) right knowledge of the cause and ending of suffering; (2) high and worthy intentions; (3) kind, frank and truthful speech; (4) right conduct; (5) right livelihood that does not injure any living thing; (6) the right effort to train oneself; (7) right mindfulness; (8) right meditation.

Each person, Buddha taught, regardless of caste, could attain *nirvana*—complete peace. He preached many sermons, urging his followers to avoid any kind of extreme action, to tell the truth at all times, to avoid violence, and the killing of other living things, human or animal. He taught that everyone can escape the evils in this life by good deeds and pure thoughts and by giving up worldly desires.

In Buddhism, there is no Supreme Being who controls life. There are, therefore, no prayers for there is no deity to whom to pray. It is ironic that the later deification of Buddha himself was so contrary to his own ideas.

Like Christ, Buddha did not write down his teachings. After his death, his disciples, in council, compiled his philosophy into books called *Sutras*.

Although Buddhism was for a time very strong in India, its

hold upon the people gradually grew weaker and weaker until less than one per cent of Indians today call themselves Buddhists. The "Enlightened One's" teachings have influenced many Hindus who accepted them and added them to their own religion. Thus, many of the beliefs of Buddhism have been absorbed by the very tolerant Hinduism.

Sikhs. The Sikhs are followers of a religion founded in the 15th century by the Hindu religious teacher, Nanak. He was called Guru ("Great Teacher"). Nanak sought to reconcile Hindus and Muslims who lived side by side with very differing religious and social ideas. His new religion drew its ideas from both Hinduism and Islam.

The Sikhs believe in one God, not many as in the Hindu religion. They do not believe in the Hindu caste system, but do believe in reincarnation. They have their own language—Punjabi. Their sacred book—*Granth Sahib*—contains hymns, rituals and stories about moral conduct. They don't cut the hair on their heads or faces, don't use tobacco or alcohol, and the men always wear an iron bracelet and a two-edged dagger.

Most of the 12 million Sikhs live in the Punjab, but they are also found in many of the larger cities of India. The Sikhs are excellent warriors. Their military history goes back hundreds of years when they first opposed the Muslim rulers in northern India, and later the British who were moving into their territory. Today they are among the best soldiers in the Indian army.

Christianity. The earliest Christian communities were established, according to legend, by the Apostle Thomas, who is believed to have preached in India soon after Jesus died. Syrian Christians in the 5th century, Jesuit missionaries in the 16th century, and Protestant missionaries from the 17th century on have also established churches and converted Indians to their faith.

Many of the 18 million Christian Indians live in southern India today.

42

Parsis. Descendants of the refugees who fled Persia for India in the 7th and 8th centuries to escape Muslim-Arab persecution can be found today around Bombay. The Parsis are devout followers of a religion founded by Zoroaster around 1000 B.C. Ahura-Mazda is their God and Zoroaster is his prophet.

The Parsis are thought to worship fire, but actually they venerate it as a symbol of purity. They bathe before praying morning and night. They do not believe in missionary work, and only a descendant of a Parsi may be a Parsi. Zoroaster taught that one's good deeds during life determine one's life after death, so Parsis are noted for their benevolence. They do not believe in burying their dead. When a person dies, his naked body is placed on the top of a Tower of Silence to be picked clean by vultures.

The Parsis were not bound by the dietary and caste restictions of the Hindus, so they adapted easily to the Western ideas brought into India by the British. Although there are only about 150,000 Parsis today, they have become successful leaders in industry, commerce and the professions. The great iron and steel plants of the Parsi Tata family are examples of the accomplishments of well-educated, hard-working Parsi businessmen.

QUESTIONS AND ACTIVITIES

MULTIPLE CHOICE TEST

In each of the following you have three choices. Choose the only correct answer.

1. The largest single religion in India today is (*a*) Hinduism, (*b*) Christianity, (*c*) Islam.
2. The Hindus worship (*a*) one god, (*b*) many gods, (*c*) no gods.
3. The highest class in the Indian caste system is the (*a*) military, (*b*) priests, (*c*) workers.
4. Vishnu and Siva are (*a*) leaders of the Muslim religion, (*b*) gods in the Hindu religion, (*c*) territories in central India.

5. The *Vedas* are (*a*) the invaders of North India, (*b*) the rulers of central India, (*c*) sacred hymns and prayers in the Hindu religion.
6. The *Ramayana* is a great epic Indian story about the (*a*) creation of the world, (*b*) founding of the Hindu religion, (*c*) adventures of a king and queen who serve as examples for human behavior.
7. A precept of the Hindu religion is *(a)* reincarnation of the human soul, *(b)* no life after death, *(c)* belief in one god.
8. The Muslim and Hindu religions are similar in that both (*a*) have a holy bible, (*b*) urge pilgrimages to holy cities, (*c*) follow the same dietary restrictions.
9. The Hindus believe that one's actions in life will determine one's future state in his rebirth. This is called (*a*) *karma,* (*b*) *dharma,* (*c*) *Rama.*
10. When a Hindu dies, his or her body is (*a*) placed in the Ganges River, (*b*) buried, (*c*) cremated the same day.
11. Gandhi regarded the lowest Indian caste as (*a*) "children of God," (*b*) the servant group, (*c*) able to help itself.
12. An animal held sacred in the Hindu religion is the (*a*) camel, (*b*) cow, (*c*) elephant.
13. The founder of the Buddhist religion was (*a*) Nanak, (*b*) Gautama, (*c*) Muhammad.
14. The second largest religious group in India today is the (*a*) Sikhs, (*b*) Muslims, (*c*) Christians.
15. The principle of non-violence is an important part of the religion in India called (*a*) Jainism, (*b*) Islam, (*c*) Parsi.
16. The caste system is (*a*) growing stronger, (*b*) weakening under the changes taking place in India, (*c*) not affected by modern changes.
17. An Indian religion that draws its ideas from both the Hindu and Muslim religions is that of the (*a*) Sikhs, (*b*) Parsis, (*c*) Jainists.
18. Unlike other great religions, Hinduism has (*a*) no one founder, (*b*) many different forms, (*c*) uniform practices.
19. A "dictionary of conduct" and a storehouse of Hindu ideas is found in the (*a*) *Vedas,* (*b*) *Bhagavad-Gita,* (*c*) *Brahmanas.*
20. Arjuna, Krishna and Sita are (*a*) important cities in India, (*b*) Indian gods, (*c*) characters in the great poetry and stories of India.
21. The most sacred river in India is the (*a*) Ganges, (*b*) Indus, (*c*) Sutlej.

22. Most Hindus (*a*) eat no meat, (*b*) are big meat eaters, (*c*) raise enough meat through large herds of cattle.

23. The caste system (*a*) is found throughout all of Asia, (*b*) was introduced into India by its Aryan conquerors, (*c*) no longer exists in India today.

24. Much was done to help the Indian Untouchables by the (*a*) great majority of Indian people, (*b*) government, (*c*) Hindu religion.

25. The number of Buddhists in India today is (*a*) less than 5 million, (*b*) more than in any other country in Asia, (*c*) growing very rapidly.

KEY WORDS OR NAMES

Can you explain or identify the following words or names? Use a dictionary or encyclopedia to find the answers.

Brahma
Rig-Veda
Upanishads
Mahabharata
Ramayana
Hanuman
reincarnation
karma

dharma
cremation
caste
scheduled class
Jainism
Gautama
Guru Nanak

COMPLETION QUESTIONS

Complete the following sentences using the names and words from the list above.

1. .... was the monkey general who helped Sita escape from the evil king of Ceylon.

2. .... was the founder of the Sikh religion.

3. .... is the name of the Supreme Being in the Hindu religion.

4. .... is the religious belief that the soul is reborn in a new body.

5. .... is the most famous collection of the sacred hymns and prayers in the Hindu religion.

6. .... is the set of rules in the Hindu religion which must be followed if a person hopes to improve his position in his next rebirth.
7. .... is the longest poem ever written.
8. .... was the founder of the Buddhist religion.
9. .... is the official term describing the former Untouchable caste in India.
10. .... is the burial practice of Hindus to release the soul.

THINGS TO DO

1. Divide the class into three committees, each to prepare a report on Hinduism, Buddhism, and Islam, including major beliefs and practices, great teachers and holy books.
2. Investigate and report to the class on "The Life of an Untouchable."
3. Contact a nearby college and invite an Indian student to your class. Ask him to tell the class about his religion. Have members of the class be prepared to compare his religion with their own.
4. Read the *Ramayana* and discuss the desirable features of human character developed in the book.
5. Arrange for the showing of a film on India, information on which can be obtained from the Consulate General of India, at 3 East 64th Street, New York City, 10021, or the Government of India Tourist Office at 30 Rockefeller Plaza, New York City, 10017.

HIGHLIGHTS IN INDIA'S HISTORY

Prehistoric Period
3000-1500 B.C.

Around 2500 B.C.—Advanced civilization flourished in the Indus River valley.

Around 1500 B.C.—Aryans invade India.

Hindu Period 1500 B.C.-A.D. 1200

567-518 B.C.—Persians invade India.

563 B.C.—Gautama Buddha is born.

326 B.C.—Alexander the Great invades India.

322 B.C.—Chandragupta founds Maurya empire.

273-232 B. C.—Asoka, Chandragupta's grandson, rules. Begins policy of religious and racial tolerance.

A.D. 320—Gupta empire (in north) founded by Chandragupta I.

380-413—Reign of Chandragupta II; extends Gupta empire.

Around 500—Huns invade India. Destroy Gupta empire.

606-647—Gupta king, Harsha, unifies much of northern India.

Muslim Period 1200-1760

1398—Tamerlane invades Delhi Sultanate.

1498—Vasco da Gama discovers sea route to India.

1510—Portuguese gain control of Goa on the west coast.

1525—Babur founds the Mogul empire in northern India.

1556-1605—Akbar, Mogul emperor, extends the empire.

1612—Trading post set up by British East India Co.

1628-1658—Reign of Shah Jahan, who builds the Taj Mahal.

1658-1707—Reign of Aurangzeb. Religious intolerance leads to decay of Mogul empire.

1757—Clive defeats the Nawab at Battle of Plassey.

British Period 1760-1947

1772-1885—British East India Co. controls most of India.

1857—Sepoy Mutiny.

1858—Br. Gov't takes over the East India Company holdings.

1885—Indian National Congress (Congress Party) formed.

1919—Montagu-Chelmsford reforms. Gandhi, Indian leader, supports self-rule and passive resistance.

1942—Britain promises India freedom after World War II.

1947—India wins independence. Partitioned into two nations.

Modern Period 1948 to Present

1948—Gandhi assassinated.

1962—Fighting between India and Communist China.

1964—Nehru dies. Lal Bahadur Shastri becomes Prime Minister.

1965—Three-week Indo-Pakistani conflict over Kashmir.

1966—Indira Gandhi becomes the first woman Prime Minister.

1971—India defeats West Pakistan in short war. East Pakistan becomes Bangladesh.

1974-75—Indira Gandhi suspends civil and political rights.

1977—Indira Gandhi resigns. Moraji Desai becomes Prime Minister.

1979—Charan Singh becomes Prime Minister. Political instability marks the year.

1980—Indira Gandhi returns to power as Prime Minister.

THE HISTORY
OF INDIA

3

(3000 B.C.—A.D. 1760)

India has a very long and continuous culture. It is possibly 5000 years old, almost as old as the ancient Egyptian and Babylonian cultures. However, unlike the latter which disappeared under the impact of foreign invaders, the culture of India, even though attacked by peoples of many religions, races and cultures, never lost its identity. Rather, it added some of the invaders' beliefs and customs to its own and thus enriched its own practices and traditions.

Let us, for the sake of convenience, divide this long history before India became independent in 1947 into four periods and study the significant features of each. These are:

1. The Prehistoric period (about 3000-1500 B.C.)
2. The Hindu period (1500 B.C.-about A.D. 1200)
3. The Moslem period (1200-1760)
4. The British period (1760-1947)

A. THE PREHISTORIC PERIOD (3000-1500 B.C.)

About 3000 B.C., civilization, in the sense of an organized system of government and developed settlements of people, grew up almost at the same time in the valleys of the Nile, Tigris and Euphrates and the Indus rivers. Much is known about the civilization of Egypt and Mesopotamia for their people left many records which scholars can read. The Indus people, on the other hand, did not keep written records although they used a form of picture writing. This, unfortunately, has not yet been deciphered. Knowledge of this Indus culture, therefore, is incomplete, although enough has been learned from the discoveries made in the last fifty years to reveal a civilization that compares favorably with those of the other two ancient civilizations.

In the early 1920's British and Indian archaeologists uncovered a city buried on the banks of the Indus River. Further excavations uncovered other towns stretching over a distance of 900 miles. The two most important cities were Harappa on the left bank of the Ravi River, a tributary of the Indus, and Mohenjo-Daro on the right bank of the Indus, some 250 miles from its mouth. It is believed that the towns and cities may have had a central government because such things as uniform weights and measures, the layout of city streets, and the bricks used in buildings are similar.

No one knows where these people came from, or how long they lived in the Indus valley. Research reveals that for some 1500 years these inhabitants enjoyed a high degree of living comfort. They carried on extensive trading not only among themselves but also with the peoples of Mesopotamia. Indus seals, emblems and other objects have been found in Mesopotamia dating back to 2000 B.C.

The towns and cities that have been discovered tell a great deal about the people who lived in them. The towns were well-fortified, carefully planned, with streets that were thirty feet wide. Each city had an efficient sewage system and public baths. The houses were made of solidly baked bricks which have not crumbled over the centuries. Many of the houses were two stories high and had bathrooms.

Most of the people were farmers who raised wheat, barley and peas. Cotton was also grown and woven into cloth and sold to countries far away. It is probable that cotton originated with the people in the Indus valley. Animals had been tamed; water buffaloes and other animals were put to work. Skilled craftsmen made pottery, bracelets, figurines and other objects from copper, bronze, gold and silver.

This civilization ended around 1500 B.C. Some scientists believe it was silted in. Others think it fell to invaders from the great steppe land stretching from Poland to Central Asia. The conquerors, a race of tall, fair people, were called Aryans. Some of their relatives invaded Europe and were ancestors of the Greeks, the Romans, the Celts and the Germans. Others were the forefathers of the Baltic and Slavic peoples.

The Aryan invasion of India was not a single action; it covered hundreds of years and involved many tribes. They made servants of the people they conquered, or drove them out of their homes into other parts of India. It is believed that the Dravidians, who are found mainly in the southern half of India, are descendants of these people who fled from the invaders.

B. THE HINDU PERIOD (1500 B.C.-A.D. 1200)

Early Aryan Culture—1500-1000 B.C. Much that is known about the early Aryan invaders of the Indus valley comes from the *Rig-Vedas,* a collection of religious literature.

These hymns paint a picture of a war-loving people who fought from horse-drawn chariots. They used a language that is called Sanskrit. They loved dancing and music, and were fond of gambling, particularly with dice. They worshipped many gods of nature. Wealth was reckoned in flocks of cattle and sheep. Their tribal chiefs were called *rajahs*; the word is related to Latin *rex* meaning "king." These were hereditary leaders, but they did not have divine powers.

The Aryans gradually overcame the inhabitants of the Indus Valley, and moved eastward across the Punjab enslaving or driving out the people then settling in villages to farm and raise their flocks.

The Emergence of the Hindu Religion—1000-500 B.C. During this period, the Aryans extended their control into the Ganges River valley, northward to the Himalaya Mountains and southward to the Mahanadi River. The great epics of Indian literature, the *Ramayana* and the *Mahabharata* are the chief sources of information about this period.

By the 6th century B.C. a society very different from the

original Aryan emerged from a fusion of Aryan and Dravidian cultures. Great gods like Brahma, Vishnu and Siva were worshipped. The concepts of rebirth, of fate (*karma*) and of duty (*dharma*) had taken form. The cow was worshipped as a sacred animal. Hinduism was being created.

Socially and politically there were also great changes. The caste system appeared. The tribal settlements of the Vedic period became small kingdoms. Cities began to grow. New trades and craftsmen such as jewelers, metal-workers, basket makers, weavers, carpenters and potters developed. Many crops including rice were raised. The king grew in power, and the influence of the religious leaders, the Brahmans, increased also. Continual fighting between rival kings prevented the creation of a united country during these centuries. Frequent warfare between the kings and the Brahman priestly class contributed to the development of new religions.

During the 6th century B.C. two new religions arose in north India. One was Jainism, founded by Mahavira (540-467 B.C.). Its central idea was *ahimsa* or non-violence. The other religion was Buddhism, established by Gautama (563-483 B.C.). With Buddhism came opposition to the caste system, and stress on the elimination of all desire as the condition necessary to escape from the evil of successive rebirths and the final attainment of the goal of *nirvana*. Both of these religious movements greatly influenced the dominant Hindu religion of the Indian peoples, and later Indian and Asiatic history.

Persian and Greek Contacts. Darius I, King of Persia, invaded northwest India about 518 B.C. He conquered the Indus valley and West Punjab regions and added them to his already large empire. Trade and commerce developed between India and Persia. Some Indian soldiers fought with the Persian emperor Xerxes when he invaded Greece in 479 B.C. Persian control over its Indian states weakened, however, and small independent Indian kingdoms were established.

Then in 326 B.C. Alexander the Great, who had conquered the Persian Empire, crossed into northwest India through one

CASE INQUIRY: Mauryan Government

The following selection is part of some principles of government suggested by Kautilya, minister to Chandragupta, the first of the Mauryan dynasty.

> Only if a king is himself energetically active, do his officers follow him energetically. If he is sluggish, they too remain sluggish. And, besides, they eat up his works. He is thereby easily overpowered by his enemies. Therefore, he should ever dedicate himself energetically to activity.
>
> He should divide the day as well as the night into eight parts. . . . During the first one-eighth part of the day, he should listen to reports pertaining to the organization of law and order and to income and expenditure. During the second, he should attend to the affairs of the urban and the rural population. During the third, he should take his bath and meal and devote himself to study. During the fourth, he should receive gold and the departmental heads. During the fifth, he should hold consultations with the council of ministers through correspondence and also keep himself informed of the secret reports brought by spies. During the sixth, he should devote himself freely to amusement or listen to the counsel of the ministers. During the seventh, he should inspect the military formations of elephants, cavalry, chariots, and infantry. During the eighth, he, together with the commander-in-chief of the army, should make plans for campaigns of conquest. When the day has come to an end he should offer the evening prayers. . . .

1. Do you consider these suggestions practical? Would they work for a head of state today? Explain.

2. What can modern historians infer from this selection about Chandragupta and the Mauryan dynasty?

Sources of Indian Tradition by William Theodore de Bary. Columbia University Press, New York, 1958, pages 246–248.

of the passes in the mountains. He helped one of the Indian kings defeat several rival rulers. However, Alexander's weary Greek troops refused to go further with him and threatened to mutiny. Alexander gave in to his soldiers' demands, loaded them into boats, and sailed down the Indus River into the Arabian Sea.

The Maurya Empire. One of the small kingdoms in northeastern India became the seat of a large empire. Chandragupta Maurya seized control of the throne of the kings of Magadha in 332 B.C. and, before his death in 297 B.C., he had conquered rival kings to the north and west of his own kingdom. He established firm rule over territory that stretched into Afghanistan on the west and to the Ganges River in the east.

The Maurya Empire was highly centralized and powerful, with a large standing army of 700,000 men and 9000 elephants, and a secret police to maintain order. Maurya's son, Bindusara (297-273 B.C.), added to the empire by conquering much of the Deccan. His grandson, Asoka (273-232 B.C.), added eastern India to the realm and ruled an empire that included much of India today.

Asoka was one of the greatest rulers in history. He spent the first few of the forty years he ruled in fighting and enlarging his empire. The more than 100,000 deaths that resulted from his conquest of Kalinga on the east coast in 261 B.C. horrified him. He gave up war and spent the rest of his life following the path of non-violence and peace. He even gave up the sport of hunting, the traditional pastime of kings. He became a Buddhist and tried to win the obedience of his subjects by kindness.

He built hospitals and rest houses throughout his empire. He had wells dug every mile beside the roads for the benefit of travelers and animals. He became a vegetarian. He had messages of tolerance and kindness inscribed on rocks and in caves.

Asoka sent teachers to all parts of his empire to spread education, and brought many students to the universities that were established in various parts of the realm. He sent missionaries to other countries. His brother helped convert the king of Ceylon to Buddhism; his daughter established a nunnery there.

Teachers were sent to Egypt, to North Africa, and to Greece.

Asoka's empire gradually fell apart after his death. His descendants were not strong rulers. Rivals challenged their power, and invaders from outside the subcontinent added to the breakdown of centralized authority. Among these invaders were: (1) the Greeks who, in the 2nd century B.C., created a kingdom that included Afghanistan and the Punjab in northwest India; (2) the Scythians, nomad tribes from central Asia, who established their brief rule over all of western India as far south as the Deccan in the 1st century A.D.; and (3) the Kushans, another central Asian people, who conquered the Scythians and native Indians and created a large kingdom in north India during the 2nd century A.D.

During these centuries of continual warfare, and the rise and fall of small and large kingdoms in northern and central India, the southern half of India was having a similar history. Petty rulers were established who continually fought each other for greater influence. The southern part of India was not invaded by peoples from the north, however, because of the tangle of forest and hill country which separated the Deccan from the upper parts of the Jumna River.

The southern part of the subcontinent was the home of the Dravidian peoples. Over the centuries they gradually divided into separate kingdoms, each with its own language. Some of the cities on the coasts of south India engaged in trade with the West, with northern India, and with the East Indies. Fine textiles, pepper, drugs, woods, ivory, and precious stones were exchanged for gold and silver.

The Gupta Dynasty. In the 4th century A.D. the dynasty (ruling house) of the Guptas arose in the north. It centered around Magadha, the old capital of the Mauryas. The first ruler, Chandragupta, was famous as a conqueror, musician and poet. His son and successor, Chandragupta II, reigned for over 40 years, and added Bengal, the upper Jumna-Ganges valley, and parts of central India to his empire. The next ruler conquered the northwestern provinces of India almost to the Indus River. The last of the great Gupta kings was Harsha (A.D. 606-647) who unified northern India.

These two and a half centuries are known as the "Golden Age" of ancient Indian history. A good deal is known about India of this period from the wealth of Sanskrit literature, the temples and sculpture that still remain, and the many coins and inscriptions that have been discovered. Two Chinese Buddhist pilgrims left records of the prosperity and good government of the empire. Fa-Hsien spent 10 years travelling around during the reign of Chandragupta II, and Huen-Tsang spent eight years in Harsha's empire.

Art, science and literature reached high peaks during the Gupta period. Sanskrit had become the official and literary language. Kalidasa, called "the Indian Shakespeare," wrote his masterpiece *Sakuntala* in the 5th century. It is the story of a king's love for a hermit's daughter, their marriage, separation and reunion. His beautiful poem, "The Cloud Messenger," tells of a lonely husband far from home who sends a cloud with a message of love to his wife.

The Indians had developed the mathematical concept of zero, and worked out a decimal system. It is probable that the so-called Arabic numerals were developed in India and were learned by Arab traders who carried the system to Europe. The value of pi (π) was determined to be 3.1416. Doctors were performing plastic surgery operations, which indicates a good knowledge of medicine. Great universities with free board and tuition were provided for talented students.

While many of the buildings of the Gupta period have disappeared, a few beautiful ones remain. There are paintings in the Buddhist caves at Ajunta in central India and at Sigiriya in Ceylon. In the practical arts the Indians were far advanced. The Iron Pillar near Delhi stands 23 feet high, is 16 inches in diameter, and weighs almost 6 tons. It was erected about A.D. 400 to commemorate one of Chandragupta's victories and has not yet rusted.

During the Gupta rule travel and trade flourished between India, southern Europe and China. Indian ambassadors represented their ruler at the Roman court. Indian and Chinese scholars exchanged visits. The influence of Indian culture on Chinese ways of thought, religion and living was considerable.

The Downfall of the Guptas.   Invading Huns, (about 500 A.D.) followed by other wandering tribes of central Asian, Turkish and Mongol people, brought about the end of the Gupta dynasty by the end of the 7th century. There was political confusion in northern India for the next 500 years.

During this period of trouble there was no unity; small kingdoms were established, fought each other and died out. Some of the northwestern states, notably those of the Rajput kings, gained considerable fame for their valiant but vain efforts to keep out the new invaders—the Muslims. With the Muslim conquest, the Hindu period of control came to an end.

India in the 12th Century.   Let us look at some of the conditions the Muslims met in India.

1. The boundaries of the many kingdoms were constantly changing.

2. The rulers were regarded as divine-right kings, with absolute powers to protect the land from invasion, and promote the "right way" of life as set forth in the sacred texts of Hinduism.

3. The government in many kingdoms owned the mines, the forests, the spinning and weaving establishments, and was responsible for the construction and maintenance of irrigation works so necessary for the farmers.

4. Hinduism was the main religion of the people although Buddhism had won many converts during and after the reign of Asoka in the 3rd century B.C. The religious tolerance practiced by many Hindu rulers permitted the spread of Buddhism, but it gradually died out in India, particularly after the 8th century A.D.

5. The influence of Sanskrit culture provided religious and cultural unity for Indians.

6. Village life was the basis of the Indian economy and way of living. A hereditary head man, usually a wealthy peasant, was in charge.

7. The land was taxed, with payments from one-quarter to one-third of the crops raised.

C.   THE MUSLIM PERIOD (A.D. 1200-1760)

In the 7th century A.D. a new religion arose in what is today Saudi Arabia. This religion, called Islam, was founded by **Muhammad.** Within a short time after his death in 632, his followers had captured Jerusalem and Damascus and conquered all of Palestine, Syria and Egypt. Within a century, Muslim armies had spread westward across North Africa into Spain and France, where they were finally stopped at the Battle of Tours in 732. Also, within the same century, other armies had pushed eastward to Bagdad and into central Asia. In 711, a young Arabian general named Muhammad ben Kasim, fought his way up the Indus Valley in what is now Pakistan, and conquered the territory. It marked the beginning of Muslim conquests in India.

For the next 300 years the chief relations between India and the Muslim rulers at their capital, Bagdad, were through trade. Personal contacts between Hindus and Muslims in ports along the southwest coast of India became more common during these years, and many Hindus were converted to Islam.

About A.D. 1000 a Turkish chief named Mahmud of Ghazni raided northern India for more than 20 years, sacking cities, destroying Hindu temples and statues of the gods, and carrying away treasures, particularly jewels. A century and a half later another invader, the Persian Mohammed Ghuri, conquered Delhi in 1193 and other important cities in northern India. He established an independent Muslim state with its capital at Delhi that lasted until A.D. 1526.

Growth of Muslim Followers.   The Muslims of India, beginning as traders on the southwestern coast, became in course of time one-fourth of the entire population. How did this growth take place?

Many conquered Hindus converted to the Muslim faith. Since government services were open only to Muslims, it was worthwhile for an ambitious person to convert. For others it was a way to escape taxes levied on non-Muslims.

Entire lower castes in some areas went over to Islam. This occurred in Bengal where caste discrimination was very severe, and it helps to explain why the Bengalis fought to establish their independence, creating the state of Bangladesh in 1971.

The Sultanate of Delhi (1192-1398). The history of this kingdom, which controlled much of northern India, is filled with tyranny, treachery, and bloodshed. Sultan succeeded sultan—34 in all. Palace revolutions replaced one another.

Some of the rulers were very capable. In the 14th century, their armies conquered parts of central and southern India, and controlled an area larger than had ever been united before.

The Mongols fiercely attacked the Delhi Sultanate. Under Genghis Khan, in the early 13th century, they overran the Hindustan plain. Under Tamerlane, in 1398, they marched into northern India and sacked Delhi. India was fragmented.

The Mogul Empire. In 1525 Babur, a direct descendant of Genghis Khan and Tamerlane, invaded India. Babur was the founder of a new dynasty—the Moguls. Before his death in 1530, Babur had conquered a large part of northern India.

Akbar (1556-1605). Babur's grandson was Akbar. Akbar's control over all of northern India and even Afghanistan was very tight. He created and supervised a strong administration. In time he controlled much of east, west, and central India. Akbar looked for the most capable people, offering high salaries. He reformed the civil service and tax collecting.

Akbar, who was a Muslim, practiced religious tolerance. He repealed the tax levied on Hindus, opened the public service to them. He himself married two princesses. Akbar encouraged learning and education throughout his kingdom.

Mogul Culture. Under the successors of Akbar, Mogul culture flourished. Great mosques, tombs, and palaces were built, and exquisite gardens were laid out. Paintings of luxurious court

This leaf from a manuscript (above) was done in the late sixteenth century during the Mughal Period of Akbar. It illustrates Alexander the Great, who crossed into India many centuries earlier in 326 B.C., being lowered into the water in a glass jar. The magnificent building below is the legendary Taj Mahal, built by Akbar's grandson, Shah Jahan, as his wife's tomb.

life and of nature studies are excellent examples of Mogul art.

Architecture and rich living reached their peak during the reign of Akbar's grandson, Shah Jahan (1628-1658). He is best known to the West as the ruler who built the Taj Mahal at Agra as a tomb for his wife. The beauty of the Taj Mahal is in the lovely curves of its marble dome, and the designs and religious inscriptions, done with costly semi-precious stones, which decorate its walls. It is said to have taken 20,000 workers over 15 years to build the memorial. In addition to the Taj Mahal, Shah Jahan was also responsible for the building of the Red Fort in old Delhi, including its palaces, audience halls, baths, gardens, and magnificent Peacock Throne.

The riches of the Shah were beyond anything known in Europe at that time. Silks from China and rugs from Persia were found on his palace's walls and floors. Gold and silver vases were everywhere. The Peacock Throne on which the Shah sat was inlaid with costly jewels. It had been estimated that the value of the Shah Jahan's treasure was worth in present values between $3 and $4 billion.

Downfall of the Moguls.   The peace and harmony that Akbar had so carefully fostered eventually ended. Aurangzeb (1659-1707), son of Shah Jahan, destroyed many Hindu temples, and earned the enmity of the Hindu Rajput princes and the Hindu population by his intolerance. He also angered the Sikhs by executing their leader. They became violently anti-Muslim, established a kingdom in the Punjab in northern India, and successfully defied Muslim efforts to conquer them.

Another group that rebelled against Mogul intolerance was the Marathas who lived in the Western Ghat Mountains on the southwest coast near Bombay. The Marathas successfully waged guerilla warfare against Mogul armies sent out to destroy them. Under their leader, Shivaji, the Marathas established a strong state in central and western India.

After Aurangzeb's death in 1707, the Mogul empire quickly fell to pieces. One province after another broke away and established independence. The Nadir Shah of Persia invaded Mogul territory, defeated its army and carried off the crown jewels and the famous Peacock Throne to Persia. Civil war further weakened the empire. In 1803, Shah Alam II came under British control. For fifty years his successors kept their title until finally, in 1858, the British sent the last Mogul emperor into exile in Burma.

The Mogul dynasty had come to an end. It was the last independent Indian dynasty. Control of India passed into the hands of the British from a small Atlantic island far away. How this was accomplished is the story of the next chapter.

QUESTIONS AND ACTIVITIES

MULTIPLE CHOICE TEST

In each of the following you have three choices. Choose the only correct answer.

1. An early civilization was established on the (*a*) Ganges, (*b*) Indus, (*c*) Brahmaputra River.
2. Two towns of this early civilization were discovered at (*a*) Delhi and Calcutta, (*b*) Karachi and Lahore, (*c*) Harappa and Mohenjo-Daro.
3. This early Indus civilization (*a*) carried on much trade, (*b*) developed iron weapons, (*c*) created a large military state.
4. The Aryan invaders of India (*a*) were defeated by the Dravidian peoples, (*b*) came from Central Asia, (*c*) conquered China.
5. *Rajah* is an Indian word meaning (*a*) god, (*b*) ruler, (*c*) peasant.
6. The Hindu religion was developed in India by the (*a*) Jainists, (*b*) Muslims, (*c*) Aryans.
7. The Persian Empire extended its rule over the Indus Valley by the conquests of (*a*) Xerxes, (*b*) Alexander the Great, (*c*) Darius I.
8. The greatest ruler of the Maurya Dynasty was (*a*) Akbar, (*b*) Asoka, (*c*) Jahan.
9. Alexander the Great destroyed the (*a*) Persian Empire, (*b*) Gupta Empire, (*c*) Maurya Empire.

10. Asoka ruled a large empire in India during the (*a*) 2nd century B.C., (*b*) 3rd century B.C., (*c*) 1st century A. D.

11. Asoka was an important king because he (*a*) was a vegetarian, (*b*) abolished the caste system, (*c*) urged toleration and non-violence.

12. The Maurya dynasty fell because (*a*) of the many foreign invaders, (*b*) there was no heir to the throne, (*c*) the lower classes revolted.

13. The "Golden Age" of Indian history refers to the (*a*) rule of the Gupta kings, (*b*) conquests of the Maurya rulers, (*c*) invasions by the Muslims.

14. The decimal system in mathematics was invented by the (*a*) Indians, (*b*) Arabs, (*c*) Greeks.

15. Education, literature and medicine made great advances during the rule of the (*a*) Persians, (*b*) Gupta kings, (*c*) Asoka.

16. Wide trade relations were carried on during the 5th and 6th centuries A.D. between India and (*a*) China, (*b*) France and England, (*c*) Spain and Portugal.

17. Although its founder was born in India and converted many Indians to its religious teachings, it is not a very important religion in India today. This statement refers to (*a*) Hinduism, (*b*) Buddhism, (*c*) Confucianism.

18. Many Hindus converted to Islam to (*a*) gain political and economic benefits, (*b*) escape military service, (*c*) avoid exile.

19. A Mongol leader who invaded and looted northern India in the 14th century was (*a*) Genghis Khan, (*b*) Tamerlane, (*c*) Mahmud.

20. The founder of the Mogul dynasty in India was (*a*) Babur, (*b*) Asoka, (*c*) Akbar.

21. The greatest of the Mogul rulers in India was (*a*) Akbar, (*b*) Kalidasa, (*c*) Chandragupta.

22. Religious tolerance toward Hindus was practiced by (*a*) Babur, (*b*) Akbar, (*c*) Aurangzeb.

23. The Taj Mahal was (*a*) a palace built by the Mogul kings of India, (*b*) an important trading center, (*c*) a tomb built by a king for his wife.

24. The Mogul dynasty was ended by the (*a*) French, (*b*) British, (*c*) Chinese.

25. Asoka and Akbar were two Indian rulers who lived hundreds of years apart yet (*a*) preached religious tolerance, (*b*) cared for the unfortunate people in their kingdoms, (*c*) both of these.

KEY WORDS AND PHRASES

Can you explain the meaning or historical importance of the following names or phrases? Use a dictionary or encyclopedia if necessary.

Guptas	Genghis Khan
Iron Pillar	Taj Mahal
Delhi	Peacock Throne
Akbar	Asoka
Mauryas	Moguls
Kalidasa	Jahan
Rajput	Marathas

TRUE OR FALSE

Do you agree or disagree with the following statements? Give reasons for your answers.

1. The Indus River civilization was an advanced culture.
2. The Maurya Empire was a highly centralized and powerful state.
3. Asoka was one of the greatest rulers of all times.
4. The Hindu and Muslim religions are very similar.
5. Buddhism is one of the largest religions in India today.
6. The Taj Mahal is one of the show places of modern India.
7. Indian contributions to mathematics were unimportant.
8. The Gupta dynasty ruled during the "Golden Age" of India.
9. The Mogul Empire was larger than the Maurya Empire.
10. Akbar was the greatest of the Mogul rulers.

THINGS TO DO

1. Using an encyclopedia, have students prepare brief biographies of Asoka, Akbar, Shah Jahan, Kalidasa.
2. Arrange a bulletin board display of Indian art and architecture.
3. The class should draw a map of India, indicating the location and size of the Maurya Empire, the Gupta Empire and the Mogul Empire.
4. Do some research and report to the class on:
   a. How the Moguls ruled India.
   b. What the archaelogists found at Mohenjo-Daro.
   c. Science and mathematics during the "Golden Age."
5. Consult the *Reader's Guide to Periodical Literature* for recent articles on Indian culture, both past and present.

63

THE BRITISH
IN INDIA

4

A. EUROPEAN INTEREST IN INDIA

Spices from Asia, tea, jewels and fabrics of silk and cotton had been known in European countries for a long time. Indian products were used in the West 2000 years ago during the days of the Roman Empire.

Spices were brought by sea to South India from the East Indies. The Indians on the Malabar coast produced pepper. From India these spices were shipped, mostly by land, through Egypt, Iraq and the Turkish lands to trading centers at Constantinople and Alexandria. From there, Italian merchants from Venice, Genoa and Pisa took them to Europe. At every place along the way tolls and bribes had to be paid before these goods were allowed to move on. As a result, the prices of spices were very high by the time they reached Europe. There, in spite of the high prices, they were in great demand.

Why did Europeans want these spices so badly that they were willing to pay a lot of money for them? One reason was their importance in preserving meats. Because there was no winter food for cows and pigs, many animals had to be killed in the late fall. However, there was no known way, except with spices, to keep the meat from spoiling. Spices were also valuable in flavoring the sour wine that was cultivated in many parts of Europe.

The Turkish capture of Constantinople in 1453 made it very difficult for the Italian traders to continue their business. The Turks placed high duties on goods coming in and going out of the city. Since the overland trade routes that had been built up over the centuries were blocked, European countries on the Atlantic coast began to look for new ways to get to India and the Far East.

Arrival of the First Europeans. The first Europeans to arrive in India and set up permanent settlements were also the last to leave. These were the Portuguese. Portuguese sea captains explored the west coast of Africa looking for a water route to the Indies. After a voyage of nearly eleven months, Vasco da Gama sailed around the Cape of Good Hope and dropped anchor in May 1498 at Calicut on the southwestern coast of India. This marked the beginning of European trade in India, and led eventually to control of the entire subcontinent by foreigners.

Vasco da Gama's first trip was followed by others. The wealth of the Indian trade prompted Portugal to send more ships, soldiers and administrators to India to establish trading posts. Alfonso de Albuquerque, between 1509 and 1515, took control of various port areas and the cities of Goa, Damão and Diu, and increased trade relations between the East Indies and Portugal.

During the 16th century, the Portuguese had a monopoly on the trade between India and Europe. Their ships brought back increasing quantities of pepper, sugar, cinnamon, rice, tea, cotton cloth and other products. Payment was made in silver or in European wines and metals. The Portuguese converted many of the natives to Christianity.

The great profits made by the Portuguese led the Dutch, the French and the English to challenge their monopoly. The Portuguese could not stand the strong competition and greater naval and military power of their rivals and were forced gradually to yield their areas of influence in India. They kept Goa until 1961.

B.   BRITISH EXPANSION

The British East India Company. The trading posts that ultimately became the centers of power in India and other Asiatic countries were not established by the governments of the European countries. They were the commercial enterprise of private trading companies established by businessmen to make money. Such a company was the British East India Company, which in 1600 was given a monopoly on British trade with India, China, and the East Indies.

The Company set up a trading post on the southwest coast in 1612. Forts were soon built at Madras, Bombay, and Calcutta. Gradually around each post a town grew up which attracted more and more Indians who worked as agents or servants. The Company was given power to sign treaties with Indian rulers, to maintain armies to protect growing trade, and to govern by itself.

Clash with the French. A French East India Company, formed in 1664, established a trading post on the southeast coast of India at Pondichéry. It carried on business with local rulers, and employed native soldiers called *sepoys.*

During the 18th century, the Mogul Empire collapsed. Independent new kingdoms under new rulers fought for power. The British and French, to strengthen their trade position, looked for allies among the warring Indian powers.

France and Britain were at war in Europe, North America (the French and Indian War), and in India. Despite the negotiation of peace in Europe, hostilities persisted in India. The French were finally defeated, and the governor of Pondichéry, Joseph Dupleix, recalled to France.

Robert Clive (1725-1774). The person responsible for the ultimate victory of the British in India was a Company clerk named Robert Clive. In 1751, when French-supported Indian rulers threatened to defeat the Company, Clive left his desk, assumed command of a small army of several hundred British soldiers and *sepoys,* and captured the city of Arcot near Madras. He became a hero over night, defeating the *nawab* in 1757.

After more brilliant exploits, Clive was appointed governor of Bengal, and for the next three years he extended British political power. In 1760 Clive returned to England and became a lord.

Meanwhile further trouble broke out. In 1765 Clive again returned to India as governor of Bengal, and built up British military and economic power in northern and central India.

Upon his return to England in 1766, Clive was accused

The Battle of Plassey (June, 1757) opened the way for British control of northeast India and made Robert Clive (top, left) a Baron. Clive's British troops (top, right) soundly defeated a combined Indian-French force, despite the Indians' use of mobile artillery (above). (Pictures: CULVER)

unjustifiably of accepting bribes from Indian princes and of amassing a huge personal fortune. He defended his actions and was acquitted. However, the trial left him very bitter, his health was shattered, and in 1774 he committed suicide.

Reasons for British Success in India.   The British succeeded in unifying all of India under one control—a feat that had not been accomplished before in India's history. The British succeeded for the following reasons:

1.   The collapse of the Mogul empire left India very badly divided and disorganized. *Nawabs* and *rajahs* fought each other for control of separate kingdoms.

2.   The British used a policy of "divide and conquer." They allied themselves with small states against larger ones; they supported one ruler against another; they played on the weaknesses of local rulers to extend their control gradually.

3.   British superiority in military and naval power enabled them to defeat larger armies than their own. They trained and equipped the native *sepoys* with modern weapons.

4.   A series of able administrators and governors introduced badly needed reforms, and improved local government services.

Later Governor-Generals.   During his term as governor of Bengal (1772-1785), and then as the first governor-general of India, Warren Hastings reformed the government of his territory. He laid the foundations for a civil service, organized a system of law courts open to all the subjects in the Company's territories, and abolished internal tariffs so that goods could pass freely throughout the area.

The Company was faced with problems from three neighboring states: Mysore, Hyderabad and the Maratha Confederacy, all surrounding the southeastern possessions of the Company. Hastings supported one then another of his opponents while allying himself temporarily with a third so that, although outnumbered, the British lost no territory. Three years after his return to England, Hastings, like Clive, was impeached for corruption in his Indian activities. He, too, was found "not guilty" after a long, bitter trial, but it cost him his fortune and his health. The Company did eventually purchase an estate for him.

It had long been the practice for Company officials to engage in businesses of their own on the side. Their salaries were low, the riches of India were vast, and the opportunities for enriching themselves were indeed great. All this ended with the governorship of Lord Cornwallis (1786-1793), best remembered as the British general who was defeated at Yorktown in the American Revolution. He reformed the civil service of the Company, prohibited the employees from engaging in trade for their own benefit, and raised salaries to make employment more attractive. As part of his reform program, Cornwallis denied to Indians the higher posts of government, in the belief that they were responsible for much of the corruption in the Company's affairs.

His successor, Lord Wellesley (1798-1805), defeated the Nizam of Hyderabad, and the Sultan of Mysore, allies of the French. He annexed the territories of several *nawabs* and *rajahs* too weak to resist him, and forced on others alliances which left them dependent on British support. By the time he had left his position, the East India Company was no longer just a trading company; it had become the strongest power in India.

The extension of Company rule into central India was continued by Lord Hastings, governor-general from 1813-1823. The western part of Nepal in the north was annexed. His successor, Lord Amherst (1823-1828), annexed Assam in the northeast, and conducted a successful war against the king of Burma.

Lord Bentinck introduced some significant Western ideas during his term as governor-general (1828-1835). English was made the official language for all Indian matters. He abolished the practice of *suttee,* according to which a Hindu widow was supposed to throw herself on the funeral pyre of her dead husband and thus join him after death. He stamped out the religious fanatics who held up travelers and strangled them to death in order to get human blood required in their worship of the goddess Kali. These fanatics were called *thugs*—a word that has come into the English language. The practice of female infanticide (the killing of girl babies) was stopped.

Under Lord Dalhousie (1848-1856) the process of British conquest was completed. The Punjab and Burma were annexed, as were the great state of Oudh, and a number of small Maratha states whose rulers died without heirs.

During Lord Dalhousie's term of office, a postal service and telegraph system were set up. Roads and railroads were constructed on a national scale. Canals for irrigation, particularly the Ganges Canal, provided a steady supply of water for farming purposes. By a law of 1854, a Department of Public Instruction was established in every province to promote elementary education in the native language and higher education in English. Girls as well as boys were to receive this education. Vocational, medical and engineering schools were improved.

Gradual Expansion of Parliamentary Control. The East India Company's power and wealth led to demands that the British Parliament take over the Company's possessions in India. In 1773 Parliament for the first time asserted the right to regulate the Company by appointing its own governor-general. In 1784 a new Regulating Act created a Board of Control under Parliamentary supervision, with authority to recall a governor-general, and to supervise all the acts which "relate to the civil or military government, or the revenues of the British territorial possessions in the East Indies."

In 1813 Parliament ended the Company's monopoly on Indian trade. In 1833 it deprived the Company of trading rights in India, leaving it as the political agent of the Crown. In 1853 Parliament ended the Company's power to make appointments, and required that entry to the service be made on the basis of competitive examinations.

C. THE GREAT MUTINY (1857)

A year after Lord Dalhousie had returned to England, the discontent of Indian troops came to a violent head. In May 1857, what the British call the "Great Indian Mutiny" and what some Indians call the "First War of Indian Independence" took place.

The revolt began in the army post at Meerut, some 30 miles from Delhi. There the Company's *sepoys* killed every European man, woman and child on whom they could lay their hands. News of this quickly spread and the *sepoys* at the army posts in Kanpur and Lucknow also mutinied.

The primary cause of the revolt was the issuing of new cartridges that had been greased with animal fat. The soldier had to bite off the end of the cartridge and pour the powder into the barrel of his gun. Since to Hindus the cow was sacred, touching the cartridges greased with beef fat was a sacrilege. Among the Muslim soldiers, it was rumored that the cartridges were greased with pork, which to them was taboo.

Another cause of resentment was the requirement that soldiers serve overseas in Burma and elsewhere, even though travel across ocean waters was regarded as wrong by upper-caste Hindus. The new railroad and telegraph construction was disturbing also, and there were rumors of enforced conversion to Christianity.

The revolt received support from many discontented elements in northern India—dispossessed princes, their unemployed former soldiers, and many others who were worried over the introduction of alien ideas and the outlawing of old Indian customs. Yet it was not a national uprising. Southern India remained loyal, and even in the north many, including the Sikhs, remained on the British side.

The mutiny was put down with great difficulty after a year of hard fighting with the help of British troops from abroad. The British suppression of the revolt was as cruel and as violent as had been its beginnings.

D. BRITISH REFORMS IN INDIA

The Government of India. When the revolt had finally been put down, the British government decided to take over the Company's empire. In 1858 Parliament passed "An Act for the Better Government of India" which transferred the entire administration of the Company to the British government.

India consisted of two parts: British India and Native India. British India, under control of Parliament, included about three-fifths of the subcontinent—the most heavily populated and productive areas. Native India consisted of about one-third of the land and about one-fourth of the population in 562 princely states. These were scattered over the subcontinent, and ranged in size from Hyderabad, as large as France, to tiny states of a few hundred acres. Some states were ruled by Hindu *maharajahs,* others by Moslem *nawabs* or *nizams.*

The princes' powers were regulated by treaties with either the East India Company or the British Crown. Some were allowed to control their own courts, schools, and even soldiers. However the British government was in charge of their foreign affairs and their relations with each other. It even had the right to supervise their internal affairs. Each native ruler was advised by a British official, a Resident appointed by the viceroy.

In 1876, by an act of Parliament, Queen Victoria was made Empress of India and ruler over the Indian princes' states as well as British India. At the head of the government was the viceroy, appointed by the British Crown, and responsible to the Secretary of State for India, and to Parliament. He governed with the help of appointed officials, mostly British. The chief posts in the Indian government were filled by men hand-picked from the Indian Civil Service. As late as 1935 only one-third were Indian.

The native peoples of British India had no voice in the government of their state or country. Elective positions were few, and no popular elections were held until the 20th century when the British began to yield to Indian demands that they control their own destiny.

This statue of a regal Queen Victoria in Calcutta serves as a reminder of the years that India was part of the British Empire.

Benefits of British Rule. During the many years of British control by Company or Crown, significant changes were brought about in Indian life, thought, and work. Among these should be included the following:

1. India, for the first time in its history, was completely unified. With this *Pax Britannica* came a greater degree of peace, law and order, relief from famine, personal freedom and political unity than the Indian people had ever known before.

2. Concrete improvements include the following:

    (*a*) The best and most extensive railroad system in all of Asia was constructed. Its 4000 miles of railroad track, in 1871, had been increased ten times by 1941.

73

(*b*) A national postal and telegraph network had been established.

(*c*) A canal system helped irrigate and reclaim millions of acres of land for agriculture.

(*d*) Public health measures against cholera, smallpox, and other deadly diseases helped lower the death rate. The population of India increased from 100 million in the 17th century to 300 million at the beginning of the 20th century.

(*e*) A famine relief system aided millions of starving people when harvests were poor. It is estimated that 20 million people starved during drought years in the 19th century.

3. New schools were started by the British, by princely governments, by missionaries, and by private enterprise. These schools were at all levels, including universities. The English language was used in all schools of higher education. Though only a tiny minority of Indians attended these schools, those who did received a fine English education (facility in English became the badge of an educated man). They studied English ideas about democracy and nationalism, and became the eventual leaders of the movement for Indian independence.

4. Law and order were established by a competent group of civil servants who conditioned the people to accept the orderly processes of government.

5. Equality before the law, regardless of religion, race or social status, became the ideal of the Indian people.

6. Certain religious and caste customs, regarded as barbaric by Westerners, were ended. These included *suttee, thuggery* (ritual strangling of people), and female infanticide.

7. Textile and jute factories, iron and steel plants were built, marking the beginning of industrialism. Shipping and banking facilities were increased. Trade with the rest of the world was expanded.

Limitations of British Rule. Many Indians believe that India's present poverty is due to the fact that the British drained great wealth from the country and used the Indian economy for the benefit of Britain rather than India.

The concrete improvements noted above, they say, were paid for entirely by the Indian taxpayers. The maintenance of the Indian army was also paid out of Indian taxes.

One of the most serious complaints against the British during their period of control was the almost complete separation of ruler from ruled. Indians were barred from senior positions in the Civil Service. The British treated the Indians as inferiors socially, morally and culturally. Indians were barred from membership in British clubs. The British attitude toward Indian customs and religions changed from disapproval to contempt. The British developed a caste system of their own, summarized by signs saying "For Europeans Only" that were posted in public places such as railway carriages, park benches and restaurants.

The small, home industries of spinning and weaving cotton cloth that had been an important way of earning a living for many Indians, were ruined by the competition of British machine-made textiles. British industry was protected against the manufactured imports of India, but no tariff was placed on British goods in India until 1921.

The landholding and tax-collecting systems helped make the Indian peasants poor. The British introduced the system of paying taxes in cash instead of in a percentage of the crop raised. When the harvest was bad, the peasant, unable to pay in cash, was faced with the prospect of losing his land. This forced him to borrow the money to pay his taxes, putting a burden on him that often remained for the rest of his life. In the northern part of India, *zamindars* (tax collectors) became landlords at the expense of the peasants in their districts. The tax collectors grew rich while the peasants became either share-croppers on land that was formerly theirs, or unemployed. Some farmers had to take jobs building canals, collecting fire-wood, or working on the land of the rich farmers as part-time workers. This system increased the poverty of the Indian people.

75

Summary. It is not easy to assess the good and the bad results of British rule in India. There were many positive achievements, as we have seen. But there were also effects from which the Indian people have not yet recovered.

However, the movement for Indian independence would not have been possible without the free press and the training in government that were allowed to exist in India. Journalists, teachers and lawyers were trained in the British universities. Indians were trained for government in the civil service, though their positions were on the lower levels. A group of fairly well-trained men could carry on government when the day of freedom came, and the new ideas of nationalism and democracy had united all Indians against British imperialism.

In the next chapter we shall relate the story of Indian independence.

QUESTIONS AND ACTIVITIES

MULTIPLE CHOICE TEST

In each of the following you have three choices. Choose the only correct answer.

1. The first permanent settlement by Europeans in India was made by the (*a*) French, (*b*) British, (*c*) Portuguese.
2. Spices were particularly valuable in the early modern period of history because they (*a*) helped in the preservation of food, (*b*) were essential for fertilization of soil, (*c*) served as food for animals.
3. Among the spices that were imported from the East into Europe was (*a*) salt, (*b*) pepper, (*c*) breadfruit plant.
4. The chief Portuguese trading port in India was (*a*) Calcutta, (*b*) Pondichéry, (*c*) Goa.
5. The first European to sail to India around Africa was (*a*) Bartholomew Diaz, (*b*) Vasco da Gama, (*c*) Warren Hastings.
6. The Portuguese were interested in Indian trade and (*a*) spreading Christianity, (*b*) opening up gold mines, (*c*) selling opium.
7. The British East India Company was a (*a*) private company, (*b*) government-owned corporation, (*c*) foreign-controlled company.

8. The British East India Company was (*a*) in competition with other British companies, (*b*) a monopoly, (*c*) owned by Clive.

9. The first British trading port in India was set up at (*a*) Pondichéry, (*b*) Calcutta, (*c*) Surat.

10. The British East India Company (*a*) used British government troops to extend its control in India, (*b*) hired its own soldiers, (*c*) brought in foreign mercenaries to serve.

11. Native Indian soldiers were called (*a*) *sepoys,* (*b*) *nizams,* (*c*) *nawabs.*

12. The leading French administrator in India in the 18th century was (*a*) Lord Wellington, (*b*) Robert Clive, (*c*) Joseph Dupleix.

13. An important victory at Plassey in 1757 led to the growth of British rule in India under the victor in that battle, (*a*) Robert Clive, (*b*) Warren Hastings, (*c*) Joseph Dupleix.

14. The British policy of allying themselves with smaller states in India against larger states is called, (*a*) appeasement, (*b*) divide and conquer, (*c*) brinkmanship.

15. The Indian practice, abolished by the British, of cremating Indian widows with their dead husbands was called (*a*) *thuggery,* (*b*) infanticide, (*c*) *suttee.*

16. Instruction in the Indian colleges and universities during the period of British control was carried on in (*a*) Hindi, (*b*) Urdu, (*c*) English.

17. Positions in the Indian government were given by the British on the basis of (*a*) Civil Service examinations, (*b*) wealth, (*c*) family position.

18. The head of the British East India Company in India was the (*a*) native ruler, (*b*) governor-general, (*c*) *rajah.*

19. As a result of the Sepoy Mutiny in 1857 (*a*) the British government took over the government of India, (*b*) the British East India Company's position was strengthened, (*c*) native control of India was established.

20. The chief cause of the Sepoy Mutiny was (*a*) the British suppression of all native rulers, (*b*) introduction of a new type of cartridge for guns, (*c*) the growth of a new religion in India.

21. The title of the British government's representative in India after 1857 was (*a*) viceroy, (*b*) governor-general, (*c*) king.

22. British India, under Parliamentary control, consisted of the (*a*) greater part of the country, (*b*) smaller part of the country, (*c*) less important areas of the country.

23. Native India, under British control (*a*) was united into one large state, (*b*) consisted of hundreds of states of varying sizes, (*c*) included a majority of the Indian population.

24. The Indian Civil Service during British control (*a*) accepted Indians and British in all positions, (*b*) excluded Indians from high positions, (*c*) favored the Muslims over the Hindus.

25. A beneficial result of British rule in India was (*a*) construction of a railroad system, (*b*) encouragement of Indian home industries, (*c*) absolute control of the native rulers in their states.

KEY WORDS OR NAMES

Can you explain the meaning or importance of the following names or terms? Use an encyclopedia or dictionary if necessary.

Vasco da Gama

"Black Hole" of Calcutta

Bartholomew Diaz

Alfonso de Albuquerque

Robert Clive

Warren Hastings

Pondichéry

"divide and conquer"

viceroy

Lord Cornwallis

suttee

thuggery

Lord Bentinck

Sepoy Mutiny

Empress of India

COMPLETION QUESTIONS

Complete the following sentences, finding the correct name from the list above.

1. .... made English the official language of India.

2. .... was the first European to reach India by way of Africa.

3. .... was the chief French port in India.

4. .... governor-general of the East India Company, was the British general defeated at Yorktown.

5. .... was the uprising of native soldiers in 1857.

6. .... established British control in India and was impeached for accepting bribes.

7. .... was the ritual strangling of victims.

8. .... was the title given to Queen Victoria in 1877.

9. .... was the title of the British ruler in India after 1857.

10. .... was the Hindu custom of the wife throwing herself on her husband's funeral pyre.

TRUE OR FALSE

Do you agree or disagree with the following statements? Give reasons for your answers. Base your reasons on what you have read in this chapter and have discussed in class.

1. Spices were valuable items of trade between India and Europe.
2. France and England were engaged in a world war in the 1750's.
3. The British East India Company was largely responsible for the establishment of British control in India.
4. The Sepoy Mutiny had serious consequences for India's future.
5. Robert Clive and Warren Hastings were empire builders.
6. A succession of able governor-generals made possible the expansion of British power in India in the 19th century.
7. India benefitted greatly from British rule.
8. The British adopted a non-discriminatory policy toward the Indian people.
9. The adoption of the English language as the language of instruction in Indian colleges and universities was beneficial to India.
10. British India was the larger and more important part of the subcontinent.

THINGS TO DO

1. Prepare a debate on the subject: "British Rule in India Was Beneficial to the Indian People."
2. Report to the class on the Indian customs and practices of *suttee, thuggery,* infanticide and others.
3. Investigate the impeachment charges against and the trials of Robert Clive and Warren Hastings.
4. Draw two cartoons illustrating British rule in India, and Indian reactions to British rule.
5. Divide the class into a number of committees. Have each committee select a different governor-general of the British East India Company in the 18th and 19th centuries and present a summary of changes and reforms he introduced.

STATES OF INDIA TODAY

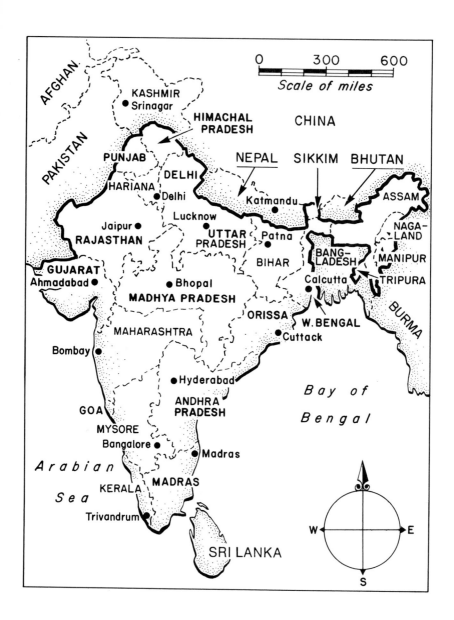

INDEPENDENCE FOR INDIA

5

A. NATIONALISM GROWS

The British helped foster Indian nationalism. They created a united India, an India in which one language, English, was spoken by all its educated people. They built its railroad system which criss-crossed the country and helped bring people together. They established a single law and a single government.

The British introduced the idea of nationalism into India through its educational system. The schools taught the Western ideas of democracy, unification and independence through courses in history and literature.

An interest in and a love of their own country were gradually awakened among the Indians. Slowly they began to think of themselves as being Indians, and became proud of their heritage whether they were Hindu or Muslim, Brahman or outcast, rich or poor. This feeling of unity was strengthened by growing resentment of the British which provided a common bond among all groups.

Formation of the Congress Party. Under the leadership of a retired Englishman, Allan O. Hume, the Indians organized an Indian National Congress in 1885. Its first meeting was attended by 70 people, most of them from the professional and intellectual class. Sympathetic Britons lent their support; three of them were elected to the presidency of the party in the early years of its history.

The Congress Party met every year in a different city and grew slowly until 1900 when its membership began to increase more rapidly. It was controlled by moderates whose chief demands were for greater Indian participation in the government, the holding of civil service examinations in India as well as in London, wider employment of Indians in the public services, and an increased educational program.

The leader of the moderates was Gopal K. Gokhale (1866-1915). As president of the Congress Party in 1905, he favored a slow, peaceful path to freedom, and supported a program of social welfare for the people.

Not all Indian leaders were so moderate in their demands. Bal G. Tilak (1856-1920), a religious leader from the Western Ghats, preached non-cooperation with the British and advocated terrorism and violence. He spent a number of years in jail because of the murder of some British officials.

Muslims as well as Hindus were members of the Congress Party during those early years and combined their efforts to secure more freedom for the Indians. However, in 1906, the All India Muslim League was created because Muslims feared the domination of the Hindu majority. The Aga Khan, hereditary ruler of the Muslims, and very well known in Europe, was influential in its formation. Sometimes the two organizations supported each other, but more often they opposed each other so that neither would become too strong in areas where religious feelings were high.

First British Government Reforms (1909). A series of events in the early years of the 20th century created much unrest in India. Epidemics of bubonic plague and influenza and droughts killed millions of people. Lord Curzon, the viceroy, increased government control over Indian universities to raise academic standards; this led to protests from disappointed students. In 1905 he partitioned the large province of Bengal to improve the efficiency of local administration. The eastern section, many of whose people were Muslims, was joined to the province of Assam. Many Hindus objected to this move and revolts broke out in which some British officials were killed.

The British Parliament decided to take action. In 1909 the Morley-Minto Reforms were adopted. These provided for an increase in the elected membership of the imperial legislative council. They also permitted separate representation for the Muslims, thus foreshadowing the later democratic development along religious lines with Hindus and Muslims voting for candidates of their own faith in proportion to their population.

Weaknesses of Indian Nationalism. The Indian independence movement before World War I was weak, not because of its moderate demands, but because of (1) the conflicts of interest between the Hindu majority and the Muslim minority, and (2) the narrowness of its base. The movement was built essentially on the Western-educated middle class whose members were more concerned with gaining political rights for themselves than in doing anything about the economic needs of the millions of peasants whose situation was getting worse and worse.

India and the First World War. Although Britain was fighting Turkey in World War I, and the ruler of Turkey was the nominal head of the Muslim religion, the Indian Muslims did not turn on the British. In fact, all classes and groups in India, with few exceptions, supported the British cause wholeheartedly. The Muslim League and the Congress Party voted loyalty. Over one million Indians served in the British army in various parts of the world. The Indian princes contributed generous sums of money to the British. From India came increased supplies of wheat and other foodstuffs for the British people.

The Fourteen Points of the American President, Woodrow Wilson, calling for "self-determination for all peoples," fired hopes for independence. The Russian Revolution of 1917, in which the despotic imperial government of the Czar was overthrown, deepened the conviction that freedom was possible.

Montagu-Chelmsford Reforms, 1919. Unrest increased and Indian leaders made more serious demands for reforms. The British answered by the adoption of the Montagu-Chelmsford Reforms in 1919.

These reforms increased the degree of self-government in the Indian provinces through a dual system known as "dyarchy."

The provincial legislatures, in which Indians were in the majority, were given control of education, agriculture and public health in their territories. A federal legislative Assembly was elected by a greatly increased electorate (5 million voters qualified). However, the British viceroy retained control over the important areas of finance, taxation, police, foreign trade and foreign policies.

Political and social unrest continued to flare up in various parts of India as demands for complete independence grew louder. To fight these "fires," the British adopted the Rowlatt laws giving judges the power to try political cases without juries, and giving provincial governments the power to intern suspects without trial. Widespread indignation and protests followed.

One such protest meeting was held at Amritsar in the Punjab in April, 1919. The meeting was broken up without warning when British troops fired on the unarmed Indians. At least 380 Indians were killed and 1200 were wounded. The massacre deeply shocked many Indians who until then had taken little interest in politics. It brought a new leader into Indian politics, Mohandas K. Gandhi.

B. GANDHI (1869-1948)

His Early Life. Gandhi was born of a Hindu family in the tiny state of Gujarat on the western coast of India. His father and grandfather had been prime ministers in some of the small states, although the family belonged to a *Vaisyja* or Hindu merchant caste. He had learned from his mother to appreciate *ahimsa,* non-violence to all living things. He was married at 13 to a girl of his own age.

At the age of 18, he left his child bride and was sent to England to continue his studies. He graduated with a law degree three years later, and returned to India. He left shortly afterward for South Africa, where thousands of Indian immigrants offered possibilities of work for a young lawyer willing to live abroad, and he stayed there until 1915. In South Africa he was

Culver Pictures

Wearing only a simple loin cloth, Mohandas Gandhi teaches his people. The Mahatma showed India and the world the power of moral persuasion through non-violent civil disobedience.

successful in furthering the rights of the small Indian minority which was being discriminated against.

Gandhi's Methods. It was in India that Gandhi put into operation his idea of mass resistance through non-violence. He called this *satyagraha* ("soul force"). This force came from Gandhi's belief that it was wrong to injure a living being; that love should be returned for hate, good for evil, unselfishness for selfishness. He believed in conquering by the power of goodness. His idea was that an opponent could be won over more surely by love, patience and sympathy than by force.

He urged a program of passive resistance and civil disobedience. He said: "Don't pay your taxes or send your children to an English-supported school. Send them to a school where they may learn their own native language. Make your own cotton cloth by spinning the thread at home, and don't buy English-made goods. Provide yourselves with home-made salt, and do not buy government-made salt." He argued for a better status for Untouchables and called them *harijans* or "children of God." "I do not want a kingdom, salvation, or heaven," he said. "What I want is to remove the troubles of the oppressed and the poor." He favored more freedom for women, a return to the ideals of ancient Hinduism, and the improvement of village economics.

He wanted nothing for himself, and asked for little. He dressed in the peasant's homespun loin cloth or *dhoti.* He became a strict vegetarian, eating barely enough to keep alive. He fasted for penance and also to secure political concessions from the British government. By his beliefs, his actions, his very life, he was considered a saint by his people. His leadership in their drive toward complete independence increased steadily after 1920.

Gandhi contributed the following to Indian nationalism: (1) He introduced the highly successful methods of non-violent non-cooperation and civil disobedience. (2) He changed the base of the movement for complete independence from a small Western-educated group into a mass movement supported by the uneducated millions. (3) He brought into the nationalist movement the concept of social justice and equality.

The Indian people called Gandhi, with great affection, *Mahatma,* meaning "great soul." Sometimes they added "ji" when speaking of him to show the respect in which he was held (*Gandhiji*). Sometimes he was referred to as *Bapuji,* meaning "honored father." Let us see how Gandhi brought about this independence of India.

Beginnings of Non-cooperation. Gandhi at first favored cooperation with the British. But after the Amritsar Massacre in 1919, he turned his back on them and embarked on a countrywide tour calling upon the people to boycott English goods, schools and courts, and to refuse to pay taxes. Millions of Indians, from peasants to students and Congress leaders, followed his lead. The movement did not succeed. Violence broke out, and Gandhi called off his non-cooperation campaign. He was promptly put in jail by the British, the first of several sentences he served.

For the next few years, Gandhi continued his efforts to teach the Indians how to use his methods more effectively. He talked, he fasted, he taught. More and more Indians listened to him. More and more of the British in India and in Britain began to realize that their days of empire in India were drawing to a close.

A sign of this was revealed in the Simon Commission Report in 1929 which recommended increased responsibility for the elected provincial legislatures and eventual dominion status for India. Because there had been no Indians on this Commission, the Indian National Congress boycotted its report, and issued a declaration of independence setting January 26, 1930, as Independence Day. It was just 20 years later that the Constitution of Free India finally came into effect. The date is now celebrated annually as Republic Day, the Indian equivalent of the American Fourth of July.

To dramatize Indian discontent with the Simon Report in a non-violent way, Gandhi said he would make tax-free salt on the seashore in defiance of the British salt monopoly. He left his *ashram,* or retreat, near Ahmedabad, and walked 241 miles in 24 days, with an ever-increasing group of followers. This march, which was reported in the world's newspapers, was followed by wide-scale and effective civil disobedience. In less than a year 60,000 people were put in jail. But the salt tax was not repealed.

Conferences were held in London which Gandhi was invited to attend. On the promise that the political prisoners would be released, Gandhi went to London. When he returned to India to learn that repressive laws were still being enforced, he resumed civil disobedience. Tens of thousands of Indians followed his lead.

This pressure forced Britain to grant further concessions to the Indian nationalists. The Government of India Act of 1935 gave complete autonomy to the provinces and created a federal system by which dominion status was to be achieved later. The franchise was extended to 35 million voters, a large increase over the previous franchise. The central legislature was to consist of representatives from British India and the princely states with wider powers except that defense and foreign affairs were to be left in the hands of the viceroy. This federal system could not go into effect without the agreement of half the princes. Their agreement was never secured so the system was never put into operation.

The Indian Congress Party won majorities in the 1937 elections in eight of the eleven provinces of British India. Muslim ministries or coalition governments were formed in the others. This led to bitter feelings between the Hindus and the Muslims. The Muslim League, under Muhammad Ali Jinnah (1876-1948), a Bombay lawyer and one-time nationalist, split with the Congress Party. Jinnah raised the cry of "Islam is in danger!" His demands for an independent Muslim state for the millions of Muslims laid the foundations for what was later to become Pakistan.

India in World War II. World War II, which broke out in 1939, had important effects upon India. The country, because of its ties to Britain, found itself at war with Germany and Japan. Indian leaders sympathized with the British cause, but refused to give official support so long as Britain was unwilling to grant dominion status to India until after the war. Many of the Congress leaders went to jail because of their non-cooperative attitude. Britain granted them freedom after World War II.

Over 2 million Indian soldiers fought bravely for the British in the war. India raised food and provided war materials for Britain. American air bases, troops and money appeared in India. This unexpected wealth enabled India to wipe out its debt to Britain. In fact, by the time the war was over, Britain owed much money to India.

New industries had been created and many of the established textile and jute mills, cotton-processing and iron-producing factories had been transferred to Indian hands. There were many new opportunities for work in factories and in the army. The peasants had more money because of war purchases for the British and American troops. This economic improvement affected the lives and thoughts of millions of Indians.

C. THE WINNING OF INDEPENDENCE

World War II ended in 1945. European empires in Africa and Asia were breaking up. The Labor Party won the election of 1945 in Britain. Clement Attlee, the new prime minister, was very sympathetic toward the idea of an independent India.

The Partition of India.　But the British faced a serious problem: whether India should be united or divided. Muhammad Ali Jinnah, leader of the Muslim League, favored a separate Muslim state to include those parts of India, such as the Punjab in the northwest and Bengal in the east, where the Muslims were in great majority. However, within these provinces there were large areas with Hindu majorities. What protection would be given to minority groups in provinces that were overwhelmingly Hindu or Muslim?

The British suggested a federation of all Indians, with local self-government in minority areas. This set off violence and bloodshed between the two groups.

The British government sent a new viceroy, Lord Louis Mountbatten, to India in March 1947. Within a few weeks he had agreed to set August 1947 as the date for independence. Since he could not arrange an agreement between the Muslim League and the Indian National Congress, he recommended that India be divided into two states—Hindu India and Muslim Pakistan.

Jawaharlal Nehru, successor to Gandhi as the Congress leader, reluctantly accepted partition although Gandhi refused to attend the celebration on August 15, 1947, Independence Day.

Mass Migrations.　Even before the division of India into two separate states was official, millions of Indians packed up their belongings in oxcarts and began to move. The Muslims sought the provinces assigned to Pakistan; the Hindus and Sikhs fled from them. Conflicts between these groups were inevitable. It is estimated that more than one-half million people were killed in these journeys, which continued for years after partition.

The migrants became a problem for both states since they

CASE INQUIRY: *The Old System Passes*

This selection is taken from the memoirs of a privileged, well-educated Indian.

> One day in 1928 my father asked me if I had decided what I was going to do after finishing college next year. To three generations of young Punjabis the unquestioned choice had been the Indian Civil Service, and I assumed that this was what my father would expect of me. I was therefore taken aback by his next question. Did I see any future in the I.C.S. or, for that matter, in Government service? I took in his point, but I was surprised that political doubt had crept in even in my father's mind. I had not expected this of his generation. . . .
>
> I think these doubts in father's mind began not from any growing political conviction . . . but from a change that was taking place in the relationship between his generation and the new generation of Englishmen coming into the department.
>
> I think father's contemporaries had learned and worked unquestioningly for long enough. At first they were grateful for the opportunity, but as time went on they became proficient at their jobs. They had grasped the opportunity well and made a success of the chance afforded them, but naturally time came when the sense of gratitude wore off and they judged themselves on their own merit. . . .
>
> Furthermore, the English newcomers were not the pioneering type of fifty years ago. As our knowledge of English grew, their facility in Hindustani and Punjabi began to diminish; the ease of travelling and the spread of amenities helped to weaken their interest in the land. . . . When the motor-car arrived, the superintending engineer could tour through his whole circle of a radius of a hundred miles or more in two days. The amenities of the headquarters towns, the club, electricity, ice and fans, made them reluctant to travel.

1. Why does the writer note the English officials' inability to speak Hindustani and Punjabi? Their attachment to the amenities?

2. Does he seem to be predicting some far-reaching change in Indian affairs? Have events since 1928 tended to support him?

Punjabi Century by Prakash Tandon. Chatto & Windus, Ltd., London, page 196. By permission of Miss Maya Tandon.

had to be housed, fed and employed. They had to adjust to their new surroundings, and pick up the threads of their old lives among strange people. The help given to them by the states of India and Pakistan was a severe drain on the resources of both governments.

Death of Gandhi.   In an effort to end the Hindu-Muslim rioting and killings, Gandhi began a fast until death. When the many leaders of the various religious groups promised that they would do their best to restore harmony and peace, he ended his fast. But the rioting and killings continued.

Many Hindus were angry at Gandhi's tolerant attitude toward Muslims and his efforts to make peace with them. A member of a militant extremist Hindu organization, N. V. Godu, assassinated Gandhi at a prayer meeting on January 30, 1948. The gentle Indian leader, who had so strongly opposed violence for half a century, died by violence.

His death was mourned by all of India and the whole world. But it did not end the troubles.

The Princely States and India.   Under the British plan for partition, the 562 states that made up India were to be joined with Hindu India, Muslim Pakistan, or remain independent according to the wishes of the ruling prince. Most of the princes were persuaded to join either India or Pakistan—whichever part was next to their own territory.

The two largest states—Hyderabad and Kashmir—had not joined with either of the new countries when Independence Day came. Hyderabad, with a Muslim ruler but a predominantly Hindu population, was completely surrounded by Indian territory. The Indian army invaded it in 1948, and it was forced to join India.

Kashmir, surrounded by both India and Pakistan, was a more complex problem. Its ruler was Hindu, its people mostly Muslim. Tribesmen from Pakistan invaded Kashmir in 1947 and India flew in troops to prevent them from taking it over. A cease-fire was arranged by the United Nations in January, 1949. About two-thirds of Kashmir remained in Indian hands, the remainder under Pakistan control.

For years the United Nations has tried to hold a plebiscite in Kashmir but has not been able to do so because of India's objections. Fighting between the troops of India and Pakistan again broke out over Kashmir in 1965. Another cease-fire, brought about by the United Nations, ended the fighting.

The New States of India. When the princely states joined India or Pakistan, they surrendered all their ruling powers in return for an annual allowance based on a certain percentage of the revenues of their states.

The boundaries of these 27 states were not drawn in a very logical or convenient way. In 1956 state boundaries were re-drawn largely on the basis of regional language. The 27 states were reduced to 14, later increased to 17. In 1971 Himachal Pradesh became the 18th state. Manipur, Meghalaya and Tripura became full states in 1972. In 1975, the Sikkim Assembly voted in favor of merging with India. The people supported this proposal and the Indian Parliament made Sikkim the 22nd state of the Union.

D. THE GOVERNMENT OF INDIA

Parliamentary System. The Indian government is patterned after that of Great Britain, but has some resemblances to the American system.

The most important official is the prime minister, who is the leader of the political party or coalition of parties that controls a majority of the seats in the lower house. He or she chooses the cabinet to help direct the different government departments such as Foreign Affairs, Education and Transportation. If the prime minister should lose the support of the majority in the Parliament, he or she must resign and a new election must be held to choose the members of the lower house. The term of office of members of the lower house is five years, which means that elections must be held at least once every five years.

GOVERNMENT STRUCTURE OF INDIA

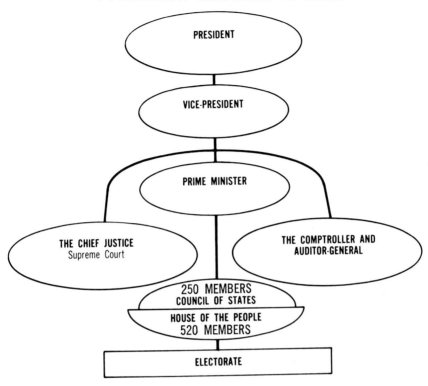

There is a president and a vice-president, each of whom is elected for a five-year term by the members of the Indian Parliament and of the state legislatures meeting together. While the position of president is largely ceremonial like that of the British monarch, actually he has under the Indian constitution power to take over the authority of the prime minister if the prime minister is not strong enough to govern.

The Parliament.   The federal legislature consists of two houses. The upper house, *Raiya Sabha* ("Council of States"), consists of 250 members. All but 12 of the members are elected by the state legislatures representing the 22 states. They serve for six years, one third elected every two years (like our Senate).

The lower house ("House of the People"), *Lok Sabha,* has 520 members elected directly for five-year terms by all adults.

93

The upper house has only advisory power over money bills. If the two houses disagree on any other bill, the final decision is reached by a joint sitting of both houses. This gives greater power to the lower house, which has twice as many members.

Another point of resemblance to the American system is the existence of a Supreme Court that interprets the constitution. To amend the Indian constitution, two-thirds of the members of each house must be present and vote. A majority of the total membership of each house is needed. Some types of amendments must be ratified by the state legislatures.

The federal government has more important powers than the individual state legislatures which also have parliamentary governments. It can create new states or abolish them, change their boundaries at will, or take over their powers. The federal government controls the major sources of revenue, foreign affairs, defense, interstate commerce, money, highways, and the incorporation of businesses.

The constitution left to the states control over the police, local government, public health, education and agriculture. Both state and federal governments have power over prices, treatment of refugees, and the control of professions. Each state has a governor, appointed by the president of India. The governor has wide powers. He can dismiss the prime minister of his state if he thinks the public interest demands it. He can dissolve the state legislature before its five-year term is up, hold new elections, and veto bills passed by the state legislature.

Individual Liberties.　The Indian constitution contains an elaborate section on the fundamental rights of all Indians. Freedom of religion is guaranteed, with special protection for religious minorities in cultural and educational matters. Also included among these rights are: freedom of speech and association, a guarantee against arbitrary arrest and imprisonment, the outlawing of untouchability, and the forbidding of discrimination of any kind because of race, religion, caste, sex or place of birth.

Although jury trials are guaranteed for all accused persons,

India has a preventive-detention law under which persons who have not yet committed a crime may be put in prison for one they are expected to commit. This law has been applied many times, most recently in 1974-75 when **Prime Minister Indira Gandhi** suspended many civil and political rights.

The Indian constitution also contains broad principles of state policy. The slaughter of cattle and the use of intoxicating drinks are prohibited. There are provisions for promoting free and compulsory education for all children under 14, protection of the health and strength of workers, and improvement of the food standards of the people.

Voting in India. There are no educational or literacy requirements for voting in India. All adults are permitted to vote. There are many political parties in India. Since 75 per cent of the voters cannot read or write, how do they know for which party to vote?

Symbols are used to represent the different parties. The Indian National Congress Party is represented by a team of yoked oxen. The *Praja* Socialist Party's symbol is a thatched hut. Other symbols are a lighted lamp, an elephant, a ladder.

Political parties are identified for illiterate voters by special symbols.

Political Problems.   Although there are more than a dozen political parties in India, the Congress Party, the largest before its split, had controlled the government since its formation until 1977. In the three elections of 1952, 1957, and 1962, it had a clear majority in the federal legislature and in most of the state legislatures.

The elections of February, 1967, were, however, disastrous for the Party. Although it received more votes than any other party, it won only a narrow majority in the federal legislature. In the state elections, the Party lost control of 8 of the 17 legislatures. Many voters cast their ballots not so much *for* an opposition candidate as *against* the Congress Party candidate. They were protesting food shortages and rising grain prices, riots in many cities, the country's stagnant economy and the fact that the Congress Party had been so long in office. In 1969 the Party suffered more defeats in local elections but retained national office.

Mrs. Gandhi called for national elections in March 1971 when she and her Congress Party won a sweeping victory. After the development of new opposition and other serious internal opposition Mrs. Gandhi invoked a state of emergency in June 1975. As a result, the opposition parties were able to merge into the Janata Party for the March 1977 elections and defeated the Indian National Congress Party. Moraji Desai, leader of this new group, became Prime Minister.

Desai's government indicated its dissatisfaction with the pattern of India's growth and its intention to emphasize rural development. In 1978 the new five year plan for 1978-83 was put into effect. During the year factionalism began to develop within the Janata Party, and the Prime Minister asked for and received Charan Singh's resignation in June 1978. The government had to deal with major flood damage in the fall.

In 1979, Prime Minister Desai's government was able to arrange treaties for cooperation in trade, as well as scientific and technological development. Yet, disagreements continued within the Janata Party. Following the resignation of 18 members of Parliament from the party, Desai resigned on July 15, 1979 rather than face a vote of no-confidence. The country was threatened with major political instability. Finally President Neelam Sanjiva Reddy named Charan Singh Premier-designate when he claimed to have the support of a majority of the members of the legislature. Singh and his government were sworn in on July 27, 1979. However, when Singh failed to gain the support of Indira Gandhi and the opposition political parties, he too was forced to resign. India found itself in political turmoil.

In January 1980, elections were held and Indira Gandhi's Congress-I Party returned to power with an overwhelming majority in both houses of Parliament.

E. INDIA'S PRIME MINISTERS

Jawaharlal Nehru (1892-1964).   Almost in every way, Nehru was the opposite of Gandhi. An aristocrat by birth, a member of a wealthy Brahman family, Jawaharlal Nehru was raised in the lap of luxury. At 15 he was sent to England for the best English education, specializing at Cambridge in chemistry, geology and botany. Then he studied law, was admitted to the bar, and returned to India at the age of 22. His father, Motilal Nehru, a prosperous lawyer, was one of the leaders in the Congress Party, but the son remained aloof from the independence movement until the early 1920's.

The Amritsar Massacre of 1919 (see page 84), followed by Gandhi's first campaign of non-violent civil disobedience in 1921, made Nehru into an ardent nationalist. He gave up his law practice and devoted all his energies and abilities to the nationalist movement. Like others, he was jailed often for his participation in the civil disobedience campaigns.

He wrote three books while in jail, the quality of which showed him to possess unusual writing talent. One of them, *Glimpses of World History,* written in the form of letters to his daughter Mrs. Indira Gandhi, the first woman prime minister of India, is a study of world history as seen through Asian eyes.

97

Look Magazine

Wide World

Jawaharlal Nehru, India's first Prime Minister (top), earned world stature as a leader in the movement for Asian independence. Lal Bahadur Shastri (left), Nehru's successor, led India through the war with Pakistan before his sudden death in 1966.

An autobiography, *Towards Freedom,* publicized the Indian side of the nationalist struggle and was widely read in many countries. His history of India, *The Discovery of India,* written from a non-British point of view, is considered to be his best book.

Nehru travelled in Europe and Asia when he was not in jail. He visited Russia, Spain, Czechoslovakia and Italy, observing the operations of both Communist and fascist political and economic systems. While he considered fascism the more dangerous evil, his sympathy for communism ended with Russia's treaty with Germany in 1939.

Pandit Nehru became president of the Congress Party in 1929, and was reelected several times. (*Pandit* means "scholar.") When independence came to India, he was the logical choice to head the new country as its first prime minister. He held the position until his death in January 1964.

During this long period, Nehru successfully led his country through the trials and tribulations of a new-born country. He guided its economy through a series of Five-Year Plans intended to improve the people's standards of living, played a leading role in the councils of the United Nations, and raised India's stature among the world's nations. We shall examine some of his work in detail in the next two chapters.

Lal Bahadur Shastri (1905-66). After Nehru's death, the Congress Party selected Shastri as their new prime minister. Shastri had been educated in India, not in England, as Gandhi and Nehru had been. He had done no travelling outside of Asia until he took over his new position, but had been active in Congress Party politics for many years and had been a member of some of Nehru's cabinets. Because he believed in a "middle of the road" policy, he was chosen as a compromise choice.

The outbreak of war between Pakistan and India in 1965 over Kashmir was an important test of Shastri's government. The cease-fire that halted the war in a few weeks was followed by a treaty in 1966 between the two countries in which Russia played a significant role in bringing the leaders of the two countries together at Tashkent in the Soviet Union. Shastri died suddenly a few hours after he had signed the treaty.

(Left) Indira Gandhi, India's third Prime Minister returned to power in the elections of 1980, (right) Prime Minister Moraji Desai, former leader of the Janata Party.

Mrs. Indira Gandhi (1918—). The Congress Party chose Nehru's daughter, Mrs. Indira Gandhi (no relation to the Mahatma) as their new leader. The choice of a woman as the head of the world's largest democratic state indicates the changes and the progress India has made since its creation.

Prime Minister Indira Gandhi has survived weakened party influence and disastrous economic conditions. By 1969, however, the Congress Party was in firmer control because of increased food production and a lowered birth rate.

Threatened with adverse court rulings in a voting law case, an opposition protest campaign and strikes, Gandhi invoked emergency provisions of the constitution in June 1975. Thousands of opponents were arrested and press censorship was imposed. After resigning from office amid charges of political corruption in 1977, Mrs. Ghandhi returned to power in 1980.

Moraji Desai (1896—). While imprisoned during the national emergency in 1975, Moraji Desai formed the coalition Janata Party to challenge Indira Gandhi. The Janata Party defeated the Congress Party in the 1977 elections and Desai was named Prime Minister. His brief term of office ended with his resignation in 1979, when the Janata Party lost the confidence and support of the people.

QUESTIONS AND ACTIVITIES

MULTIPLE CHOICE TEST

In each of the following you have three choices. Choose the only correct answer.

1. The Indian Congress Party was founded (*a*) after independence had been won, (*b*) to fight for Indian independence, (*c*) solely by Indian nationalists.

2. By the Morley-Minto Reforms of 1909 (*a*) voting rights were granted to all Indians, (*b*) Muslims were permitted separate representation in the legislature, (*c*) the legislature was selected by Indian voters.

3. During World War I (*a*) all classes and groups in India supported Britain, (*b*) the Muslim League opposed Britain's efforts, (*c*) Gandhi objected to British discriminations.

4. "Dyarchy" refers to the (*a*) dual system of local and federal government adopted for India in 1919, (*b*) formation of the Muslim League, (*c*) reform of education in India.

5. Political and social unrest in India in 1919 was answered by the British through the (*a*) outlawing of the Congress Party, (*b*) suspension of jury trials for accused persons, (*c*) abolition of representative government.

6. Gandhi's doctrine of *ahimsa* (*a*) urged Indians to boycott British elections, (*b*) favored industrialism in India, (*c*) was opposed to violence.

7. Gandhi favored (*a*) passive resistance, (*b*) active support of the British, (*c*) a separate state for the Hindus.

8. Gandhi's program included (*a*) civil disobedience, (*b*) payment of taxes to the British, (*c*) the buying of British goods.

9. The term *Mahatma* means (*a*) cooperation, (*b*) "great soul," (*c*) violence.

10. Gandhi used fasts to (*a*) lose weight, (*b*) gain concessions from the British, (*c*) oppose the Muslims in India.

11. By the Government of India Act of 1935 (*a*) the vote was extended to all Indian adults, (*b*) a limited form of government was adopted for India, (*c*) independence was granted to India.

12. The leader of the Muslim League was (*a*) Muhammad Ali Jinnah, (*b*) Jawarhalal Nehru, (*c*) Gopal K. Gokhale.

13. During World War II, the leaders of the Indian Congress Party (*a*) refused official support to the British cause, (*b*) were jailed because of their non-cooperation, (*c*) helped Britain's enemies.

14. The Indian subcontinent (*a*) became a united independent state in 1947, (*b*) was divided into the independent states of India and Pakistan, (*c*) split into many small free states in 1947.
15. The native Indian rulers (*a*) retained control of their states after independence, (*b*) joined either India or Pakistan on a voluntary basis, (*c*) were forced to join India.
16. There are at present (*a*) 14, (*b*) 22, (*c*) 27 states in India.
17. The president of India is (*a*) elected directly by the voters, (*b*) chosen by the prime minister, (*c*) elected by the national and state legislatures of India.
18. The real ruler of India is (*a*) the viceroy, (*b*) the prime minister, (*c*) the president.
19. India has a bicameral legislature. This means (*a*) a legislature of two houses, (*b*) equality between the legislative and executive branches, (*c*) a legislature responsible to the president.
20. The ruling political party in India today is the (*a*) Congress Party, (*b*) Janata Party, (*c*) Socialist Party.
21. The prime minister who resigned after only one month in office in 1979 was (*a*) Moraji Desai, (*b*) Lal Shastri, (*c*) Charan Singh.
22. The great majority of the Indian voters (*a*) cannot read or write, (*b*) are literate, (*c*) have graduated from grade school.
23. Political parties in India are represented on the ballot by (*a*) symbols, (*b*) names of leaders, (*c*) numbers.
24. *Glimpses of World History* was written by (*a*) Mohandas Gandhi, (*b*) Pandit Nehru, (*c*) Lal Shastri.
25. The Indian Supreme Court, like the American Supreme Court, has the power to (*a*) amend the constitution, (*b*) elect the president, (*c*) interpret the constitution.
26. Indian states were created mainly because of (*a*) geographic features, (*b*) language, (*c*) religion.
27. The first prime minister of independent India was (*a*) Nehru, (*b*) Jinnah, (*c*) Gandhi.
28. Many civil and political liberties were suspended in 1974 when Prime Minister Gandhi invoked the (*a*) tenth amendment, (*b*) sedition law, (*c*) preventive-detention law.
29. Gandhi belonged to the merchant class, Nehru was a member of the (*a*) Untouchables, (*b*) military, (*c*) Brahman caste.
30. As a result of World War II (*a*) Britain owed India a lot of money, (*b*) India owed Britain a lot of money, (*c*) India was conquered by the Japanese.

KEY WORDS AND PHRASES

Can you explain the meaning or importance of the following words or people? Use a dictionary if necessary.

Indian Congress Party
dyarchy
non-violence
federal government
Mahatma Gandhi
civil disobedience
dominion
prime minister
Morley-Minto Reforms
Rowlatt Bills
Government of India
   Act of 1935
preventive detention
Pandit Nehru
Charan Singh

"salt march"
Muhammad Ali Jinnah
Swatantra Party
Government of India
   Act of 1919
Amritsar
Lord Louis Mountbatten
Praja Socialist Party
satyagraha
"harijans"
Native India
Lal Shastri
Mme. Indira Gandhi
Moraji Desai

COMPLETION QUESTIONS

Complete the following sentences, finding the answer in the list of names and terms above.

1. .... was the last British viceroy in India.

2. .... was the first prime minister of an independent India.

3. .... is the coalition political party which came to power in India in 1977.

4. .... was the method used by Gandhi to secure freedom for India.

5. .... is the first of the British laws that helped prepare India for independence.

6. .... is the term used to describe the dual government system for India set up in 1919.

7. .... is the term used by Gandhi in referring to the Untouchables.

8. .... was the first woman prime minister of India.

9. .... was the leader of the Muslims in India.

10. .... status describes India's relations to the British Commonwealth.

TRUE OR FALSE

Do you agree or disagree with the following statements? Give reasons for your answers.

1. British policies in India helped create Indian nationalism.
2. The British helped prepare the Indian people for eventual independence.
3. The Congress Party in India was always under the control and influence of the Indian upper classes.
4. India was of little help to Britain during World War I.
5. The civil rights movement in the United States learned a great deal from Gandhi's non-violent methods.
6. Passive resistance and civil disobedience were opposed by Gandhi.
7. Gandhi and Nehru were agreed on methods and goals for their people.
8. The political unity of the subcontinent was prevented by the Muslim League.
9. World War II had little effect on Indian nationalist leaders and the movement toward independence.
10. There are both resemblances and differences between the governments of India and the United States.
11. The exchange of Hindu and Muslim populations after partition was accomplished in a peaceful and orderly way.
12. Gandhi died as he had practiced while living.
13. All of the native Indian states accepted union with India willingly.
14. The boundaries of India's states were created on an unusual basis.
15. Mrs. Gandhi's state of emergency continues unchallenged.

THINGS TO DO

1. Prepare a bulletin board display of elections in India, showing: (a) the symbols used by the parties, (b) polling places, (c) the counting of the votes, (d) electioneering practices.

2. Debate the topic: "Britain created and stimulated Indian nationalism."

3. Construct a political cartoon or poster that could have been used to illustrate Mrs. Gandhi's power.

4. Conduct a round table discussion on the topic: "The Indian Government resembles that of the United States."

5. Write a newspaper article describing (a) Gandhi's salt march, (b) the assassination of Gandhi, (c) the departure of the British from India.

6. Investigate, using the *Reader's Guide to Periodical Literature* for articles, and report to the class about the mass migrations of Hindus, Muslims and Sikhs after partition.

7. Read one of Nehru's books (such as *The Discovery of India* or *Towards Freedom*) and report to the class on his activities as a leader.

8. Write a report on Gandhi's work against discrimination in the Union of South Africa. Consult a biography of Gandhi.

9. Prepare a chart to show the results of the most recent elections in India.

10. Compare the American Bill of Rights with the individual liberties guaranteed in the Indian constitution.

INDIA'S ECONOMIC AND SOCIAL PROBLEMS 6

India has a very high potential for industrial and electric power development. There are large deposits of high-grade iron ore and coal, important reserves of bauxite (from which aluminum is made), atomic materials like thorium, and large deposits of manganese and mica. The great rivers offer the possibilities of enormous hydro-electric power. India's railroad system is the largest in all of Asia. It has more irrigated land than any other country in the world. Its population of 626 million people is the second largest in the world.

According to American standards, India is still one of the poorest countries in the world. The average annual income, about $160 in American money, is much lower than most countries. However, the purchasing power of money in India is greater than the average annual income of a similar family in the United States. About two-thirds of the Indian people cannot read or write. Their diet is inadequate in quantity and quality. Gandhi once said that the Indians are faced with "an everlasting fast." The great majority of the people lack proper housing, medical care and education, in addition to food and opportunities for work.

Why do these paragraphs seem to contradict each other? Let us examine some of the serious problems that India faces today.

A. AGRICULTURE

Farming is the most important single occupation of the Indian people. More than 70 per cent of the Indians are farmers who till their small plots of land in the same way their ancestors before them did. Yet the amount of food they raise is not enough for the ever-increasing population.

Many Indian farmers still use the centuries-old method of letting the wind separate chaff from grain.

Look Magazine

Backwardness of Agriculture. There are many reasons for this serious food problem.

1. The Small Farms. India's millions of farms are very small; many of them are no more than 2 or 3 acres in size, the average being about 7½ acres. Much of the food the small farm produces—the milk, grain, vegetables and fruits—is eaten by the farmer and his family, leaving very little as a surplus for the city inhabitants.

2. Primitive Tools. Most farmers use a short-handled hoe, and a wooden stick (sometimes with an iron tip) to break the ground for seeding. The steel plow is used on very few farms. The smallness of the farms makes it impossible to use tractors, harvesters or other modern machines that have helped increase food production in other countries of the world.

3. Low Productivity Per Acre. Indian farmers are faced with plant diseases and animal pests (rats) that destroy part of their crop every year. Farmers do not have enough storage room to keep their grain safely. The soil is worn out because of inadequate fertilizer and cattle eat the crop. Many farmers do not have enough water to irrigate the land.

As a result, Indian farmers raise only one-third as much rice per acre as the Japanese farmers, or one-half as much wheat per acre as American farmers.

4. Unwillingness of Farmers to Adopt New Methods. Many Indian farmers are unwilling to try new methods, new seeds, and new tools. It would upset their ways of life too much and too quickly. If they had steel plows to use, the village carpenters and their families would be out of work with no wooden tools to make. New types of wheat seed might produce stalks too tough for their cattle to chew, or too weak to hold the grain. When American wheat was introduced, the Indians didn't like its looks and its taste. It was so different from their own type of wheat that they didn't want to raise it or eat it.

5. Heavy Debts of the Farmers. Many farmers are in debt to money-lenders or rich farmers in the neighborhood. Previous crop failures forced them to borrow money to buy seed, food and clothing. The high interest rates charged by the village money-lenders are a great burden to the poor peasants.

Economic Planning. Shortly after India won its freedom, the government decided to increase food production, develop industries and raise the standard of living of the people through programs of economic planning—a series of Five Year Plans.

Although India borrowed this idea of economic planning from the Soviet Union, it was carried out by democratic not dictatorial means. The programs, covering agriculture, industry, education, irrigation, housing, and public health, were drawn up by groups of experts from the central government, from the state governments and from private groups. They were discussed, changed and finally submitted to the Indian Parliament for its final decision. It took months, sometimes years, of preparation and debate before a program was accepted. The first Five Year Plan was adopted in 1951.

This Plan, with $7 billion to spend, concentrated more than a third of the money on increasing food production and building irrigation projects. A Community Development Program was designed to educate and persuade Indian farmers to improve their farming methods. As a result, food production increased by some 4 million tons and the program was declared a success.

The second Five Year Plan (1956-61) spent almost $14 billion, most of it on developing industries and electric power. Food production increased again under the second Plan, but at a lower rate than under the first.

The third Plan (1961-66), involving almost $22 billion, was to raise national income, increase grain production, speed industrial growth and build power projects. The wars with China (1963) and with Pakistan (1965), however, interfered with this plan because more money was needed for defense.

The fourth Plan (1966-71) and the fifth Plan (1971-75) were quite successful, and the sixth Plan originally planned for 1975-79 was terminated in 1978 in order to introduce a more intensive economic redevelopment scheme for the seventh Plan (1978-83) which was approved in March 1978.

Where does all this money come from? The government provides from 40 to 70 per cent and the remainder comes from foreign loans and investments. Taxes have been raised repeatedly but they do not produce the money needed to finance the government programs. An income tax is levied on all nonfarming incomes over $400 a year for single persons and $700 for couples. While there is no income tax on agricultural income, there is a heavy land tax.

The accomplishments of economic planning in agriculture have been impressive. Though yields per acre are still low, agricultural production has risen as these figures show:

Year	Food Grains (millions of tons)	Cotton (millions of bales)	Sugar Cane (millions of tons)
1950–51	50.0	2.9	5.6
1977–78	125.4	7.1	18.6

These figures, however, do not tell the whole story. Population is increasing. Farmers must learn to use better seed, better tools, better drainage and soil conservation, more irrigation, more fertilizer and more protection from animal pests and plant diseases. In experiments in various parts of India, production went up 100 per cent. This shows what can be done. However, tools, fertilizer, and irrigation all require money. It also takes time to train workers to educate the peasants.

Rural Reform Programs. Since independence the government has been attempting to increase agricultural production with the voluntary cooperation of the peasants. Among the programs begun during the 1950's were community development, land reform, irrigation projects and establishment of cooperatives. They were continued during the 1960's and have been the basis for further advances in recent years.

Community Development Programs. The Indian government is trying to raise agricultural production with the voluntary cooperation of the peasants. This is the main aim of a great educational program known as Community Development. It began on October 2, 1952, the 83rd anniversary of Gandhi's birth. Beginning with 25,000 villages, most of India's 500,000 villages have been drawn into the program.

Rural India was divided into over 5,000 blocks. Each consisted of about 100 villages with an area of 150 to 200 square miles and a population of from 60,000 to 70,000. A block officer or *gram sevak,* who had been specially trained ran each block, assisted by advisors on agriculture, public health, rural industries, animal care and cooperatives. The block officer tries to convince the villagers to adopt newer methods.

In 1957, a democratic reform was introduced where by each village elected a *panchayat* or council, and from this council a representative was elected to the block *panchayat.* The government provides advice, materials and money; the *panchayat* decides what changes should be introduced. This democratic planning on the village level is an effort to revolutionize Indian agriculture and thereby improve the Indian peasants' way of living.

The Community Development program worked to dig new wells to provide clean water, to construct thousands of miles of new roads, and to improve old roads thus providing better transportation and ending the isolation that has been so long a feature of peasant life. Many tools and materials have been distributed. A new hopeful attitude has slowly developed among the farmers of rural India.

Land Reform.   At the time of independence, much of the farm land was held by a small number of absentee landlords, large landholders and *zamindars,* former tax collectors who had been given, by the British, ownership of the land on which they collected taxes. As many as 25 per cent of the Indian peasants did not own any land at all. Others owned very small farms; still others were tenants. This system of landholding was a very serious obstacle in the way of agricultural improvement.

In 1953, the central government deprived the *zamindars* of their land and paid them over one billion dollars for their holdings. This land was distributed among the farmers who now pay taxes to the government instead of the rent they formerly paid to the landlords. However, the government could not reform the landholding system further because it did not have the money and because the states are really in charge of land reform.

In the 1970's the government decided to limit family land holdings to between 4 and 7 *hectares* (a hectare is about two and a half acres) if it has enough irrigation to produce two crops per year; and 11 hectares if it has irrigation for only one crop per year; and 22 hectares for all other categories of land. The average family consists of a husband, wife and three children. It is possible for larger families to obtain more land up to a maximum of two times the limit. The average size of farms is 2.63 hectares.

A solar grain dryer designed to increase India's foodgrain storage capacity.

United Nations/Ray Witlin

Irrigation Projects. During the 1970's the central and state governments placed high priority on increasing irrigation, multiple cropping, fertilizer use, and high yielding seed varieties in order to improve the productivity of the land. In addition institutional credit has been granted to the farmers and educational information disseminated through extension services. India is slowly reducing its dependence on the monsoons.

Two crops a year can be raised in most areas if water is available during the dry season. For this reason, irrigation is vital in the efforts to increase food production. When India gained its independence, there were 50 million acres of land under irrigation—more than in any other country in the world. Since then the government has built many other irrigation projects to bring more and more land under cultivation. Each of the economic plans has included provisions for this program.

One of the most spectacular is the Bhakra Nangal project on the Sutlej River in the Punjab in northwestern India. Its 740-foot-high dam—one of the highest in the world—and its 652 miles of canals irrigate 5 to 6 million acres of land.

The Great Indian Desert, some 80,000 square miles of arid land, is to be irrigated by the construction of dams. Trees will be planted and crops suited to arid soil, such as millet, will be raised.

Ten years after independence, some 20 million acres had been brought under irrigation. Local irrigation programs include the improvement of field wells, the digging of deep wells to 200 feet or more, and the use of gasoline engines instead of oxen to bring up water. Over 4000 such wells have been built in India in recent years.

Peasant indifference or opposition to the new projects is being overcome slowly and gradually. In northern India, farmers have increased the use of diesel or electric pumps to bring up water for their lands. It is much cheaper than the old *charsia* or waterwheel, driven by yoked oxen or bullocks, which raised or lowered water slowly and painfully. In other parts of India, the peasants are more slow to adopt these or other simpler irrigation techniques or use new forms of seed. However, progress is being reported.

The New York Times

A Peace Corps volunteer on a fish farm in India, advises a local farmer (above) on fish-harvesting technique. India is experimenting with this and other methods of scientific farming (below) in order to provide food for its growing population.

United Nations   United Nations

Establishment of Cooperatives. To establish larger farms on which better tools and improved techniques could more easily be used, the government has actively promoted the formation of cooperatives. It has persuaded individual farmers to combine their small holdings and has given them much help if they did so. Over 200,000 of these cooperatives were established in the early 1960's. They are service-cooperatives rather than the types found in Western countries. The government provides credit, fertilizer, marketing assistance, storage facilities and other help to the members. They are often run by officials who are paid by the government; this brings the cooperatives more closely under government supervision.

But attempts to form collective farms through the pooling of land for joint cultivation is meeting with much resistance from the farmers who feel deeply about their own plots of ground, small though they may be.

Summary. In the past 30 years, India has increased its food grain production fivefold, and doubled its industrial production. The challenge in the 1980's will be in easing the problems of labor unrest, increasing output in the major industrial plants, and providing adequate supplies of energy to both the factory and the farm. Transportation problems such as port congestion and poor road and highway conditions also need to be remedied.

Food Problems. India's food needs far exceed agricultural production every year, so the government must import food to feed its ever-growing population. Although the United States and the Soviet Union provide millions of tons of wheat and other grains on an annual basis, and other nations have stepped up their aid with food products, malnutrition and famine continues to be the major obstacle to India's growth.

Drought and subsequent famine plagued India from 1965-67 and returned in 1972-75. Since 1975 there has been much rainfall which caused even flooding. When the monsoons failed severe food shortages occurred and millions of Indians faced starvation. The United States sent some 10 million tons of wheat in 1966-67. With additional help from other countries, starvation was averted. The concentrated efforts of the government to introduce new strains of rice and wheat, together with increased use of chemical fertilizers and improved irrigation techniques increased the grain crop of India. Adequate rainfall in 1977 led to the production of almost 126 million tons. More fertilizers have been imported and produced domestically.

Because the Indian government was forced to spend more money on food purchases than planned, it meant reducing funds for housing and education. The Congress Party, long dominant in Indian politics, was accused by its rivals of inefficiency and lack of planning for such emergencies. Relations between the central and the provincial governments were strained because grants of money and supplies to the provinces were limited by the available funds. Increases in food prices, inflationary threats and the challenges to the repressive regime as well as the changes in the government made the Indian political picture more confused than ever.

B. POPULATION GROWTH

Some experts argue that India's greatest problem is its population. The ever-growing Indian population has increased overcrowding and food needs, and magnified the shortcomings in housing, health services, and education.

Every year India adds more than 13 million people to its population—people who need a place to live, food to eat, and work to do. This is like saying that a city the size of Greater New York is added to India every year. Since independence the population of India has grown by 220 million people! That is more than the individual population of all but a half dozen countries in the world!

This rapid increase of population has been due mainly to successful public health measures. Better medical facilities have decreased infant deaths. Epidemics, such as malaria and smallpox, have been controlled. The great increase in population makes the problem of economic development even harder. It makes maintaining the present low standard of living difficult.

Most Indians are not opposed to family planning, but children, particularly boys, are greatly desired by the Hindus. Such attitudes are very slow to change. The government is conducting extensive publicity campaigns for birth control. Many clinics where information may be secured are maintained and birth control devices are distributed free of charge.

However, the government announced in early 1976, that after 24 years, only 17.5 million couples of a total of 103 million in the reproductive ages of 15 to 45 years use contraceptive devices. As a result, many cities have announced plans to penalize government employees and residents who do not limit their families to two children. A plan under effect in New Delhi provided incentives to couples with one sterilized spouse or with one who has signed a pledge to undergo sterilization after having two children. Penalties curtailed a couple's access to almost all government assistance—from government jobs and housing to loans, medical care, schools and drinking water. Some states even fined and imprisoned couples who failed to comply.

Recently, the Indian government has altered its position on birth control and family planning. Voluntary family planning is now stressed. However, for the foreseeable future India will remain seriously overpopulated.

C. INDUSTRIAL GROWTH

Expansion of Industry. Before independence, British industries were turning out consumer products such as cement, rubber, leather, glass and paper. Coal mines, steel plants, cotton textile and jute mills were in operation. Under the impetus of World War II, there was greater expansion. New industries produced chemicals, bicycles, sewing machines, diesel engines and machine tools. Shipbuilding and aircraft plants were built. Since the war there has been considerable expansion of existing industries and the development of new ones. Automobiles, locomotives, electronic equipment, radios, rayon, razor blades, air conditioners and fertilizers, in addition to many machines and machine tools are now being made.

Under the Five Year Plans, the government devoted increasing amounts of money to speed up industrialization. The large steel concern, owned by the Tata family, was encouraged with government assistance to expand its production. New steel plants were built at Oussa (with the help of West Germany), at Durgapur in West Bengal (with British aid), at Bhilar, in Madhya Pradesh (with assistance from Russia), and at Bokaro. As a result, India is the third largest steel-producing country in Asia, just behind Japan and Communist China. India boasts that it produces steel more cheaply than any other country in the world.

The increase in steel at low cost has greatly stimulated small

An instructor at the Vocational Training Institute in Madras demonstrates welding techniques to a class of trainees.

United Nations/T. S. Satyan

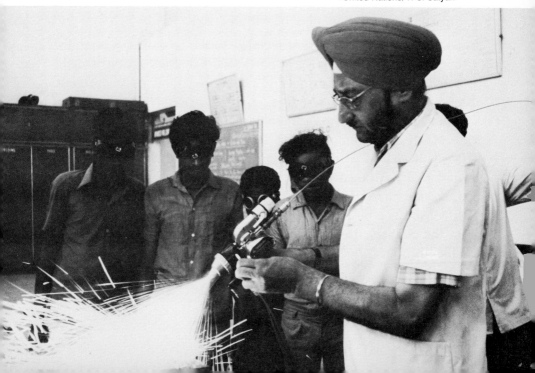

industry. Plants have been established to make bicycle parts, cardboard boxes, matches, shoes, carpets, preserved foods and many other items. They employ from ten to fifty workers, and use simple machinery. In many instances, the government helps such companies by giving them electric power at cheap rates, floor space in factories at low rentals, and by paying for the training of workers.

"Cottage industries"—handicrafts of many kinds including spinning and weaving—are still found in large numbers throughout the country. All the members of a family carry on these ancient industries in their own homes. There are probably more people engaged in earning their living by cottage industries than in any other economic activity except agriculture. They, too, receive government help, particularly in the sale of their products.

India's industrial output has increased dramatically in the last 25 years. However, it should be remembered that India is still basically an agricultural country. Mining and manufacturing account for only one-fifth of the national income of $101 billion. About 5.2 million workers are employed in large and small industries while more than 20 million people are engaged in "cottage industries." The United States is trying to persuade Indians to invest more funds in agricultural development than in industrial development to overcome their food crises.

Socialism in India.   In principle, India is called a socialist country. Its leading political party, the Congress Party, is dedicated to government ownership of industry, and its leaders talk of building a socialist society. Actually, private enterprise accounts for 90 per cent of the national income.

Much of the industry that requires large amounts of capital is in the hands of the government. Some industries have been nationalized (taken over by the government). It now owns the railroads, the telephone and telegraph services, the airlines, the life insurance business, the power industry and the largest banks in the country. It has joined with private investors to develop steel production, machine tool manufacturing and fertilizer processing. However, small factories generally remain as private enterprise. Thus, Indian socialism is very different from the Russian or Chinese concepts of socialism. In those countries almost all of industry, big and small, is in government hands.

Financing Industrial Growth. Raising the money to carry through ambitious programs for industrial and agricultural growth is proving to be a very difficult task for India. Its total annual budget of over $14 billion is slightly more than that for New York City! Defense expenditures have gone up greatly since the Chinese and Pakistan aggression incidents, and the Bangladesh war and now take up almost half the budget. India depends increasingly on aid from other countries.

The United States has, since 1951, contributed over $7 billion in gifts and loans, much of it in the form of wheat and rice. Private American foundations, like the Ford and Rockefeller Foundations, have spent over $50 million to improve the health, education and welfare of the Indian people. American companies have invested over $200 million in Indian industries, mainly oil refining and distribution.

The World Bank and the International Finance Corporation and Development Fund have loaned India over $1 billion, mostly for transportation, communications, and power supplies. The U.S.S.R. has loaned India over $1 billion, much of it for steel plant construction. Other countries that have given financial aid—a total of $950 million—include West Germany, Britain, Japan, Canada and France. Help from all these countries and institutions must be continued, and even increased, if India is to continue to develop.

Water Power. India's high potential of water power to generate electricity, so important for industry as well as for the consumer, has not yet been developed. India's power production is about 40 million kilowatt hours. Almost two-thirds of this electricity is used by industries, leaving very little for the public.

To develop their water resources, Indians have dug irrigation ditches by hand (above) and have built large dams like the one at Tilaiya (below), which provides water storage and hydro-electric power, not to mention a lake for fishing.

The government's irrigation projects will eventually increase hydroelectric power. But manpower and animal power will continue to provide much of the energy required in India for years to come.

D.   EDUCATION IN INDIA

The Indian constitution declares that all children should have free and compulsory education to the age of fourteen. Since Independence Day, the leaders of India have made great efforts to reach this goal, but it has not yet been achieved. Today, about 75 per cent of the people cannot read or write. The problems that have to be solved before India becomes a literate nation are many and serious.

Indian Education Under the British.   Before the British became the rulers of most of India, education was almost entirely religious. There were no schools for the masses. Whether Hindu or Muslim, the children of the rich were instructed by private teachers.

Under British rule, mission schools and colleges were gradually established. The British East India Company contributed money for education which was based on the English type of schooling, with instruction in the English language. When the famous historian, Thomas B. Macaulay, was in the employ of the Company, he had made English compulsory. Various other governor generals gave money only to colleges that taught in English. In fact, the Company ruled that Indians educated in English-type colleges would be given preference in government jobs. For the next hundred years, this idea dominated higher education in India.

Very little was done about elementary and secondary schooling. The few children who did go to the mission schools in various parts of the country did not stay for more than four years. Only a handful of students from the lower classes continued their education through the university.

Control of Education in India.   Education is supported and controlled by the various 22 states, much as in the United

CASE INQUIRY: "The Exam"

The following excerpt expresses the author's point-of-view regarding the aim of education in India—the all-important Exam.

Play may be an uncharted land to the children of India, one where they may discover new games, create new fantasies. The path of education, though, is littered with very explicit signposts: Read this as if chanting a charm. Write this even if you don't understand. Memorize the Correct Answers to questions. Above all, pass The Exam.

The Exam is the end-all of Indian schooling. Coming after ten years in some places, eleven years in others, it shapes all the days, all the minutes, in the schoolroom from Class One onward. It is state-administered, something like the Regents exam in New York. But . . . the graduation examination in India includes all the work the children have covered in all their school years.

Though The Exam is the same throughout each state, the style of education varies greatly from the one-room village primary school to the multistoried high-tuition education factories filled with the children of the rich in Delhi, Bombay, Madras and Calcutta.

Rich urban private-school student and destitute villager, both spend final days of preparation pacing their rooms memorizing "correct" answers, which appear in the published texts of old exams. All questions are essay style, and all answers are lengthy. An examinee therefore crams his head with hundreds of thousands of words in the hope that enough of the questions whose answers he has memorized will appear on The Exam to give him a passing mark. Rote is the ideal; original thought is frowned upon. Who knows whether the examiner will recognize an *original* correct answer as being correct?

Passing marks on The Exam qualify the student to enroll in the university. There he meets a system identical to the one he has just left. Again he must make an irrevocable commitment to a certain subject. . . And again over all his work looms the specter of the examination he must pass to win his B.A. degree.

1. Why is The Exam more important to Indian youth than other evaluations of their education?

2. According to the author, what effect does the educational system have on Indians? Do you agree? Why or why not?

3. How would you change the educational system in India?

Bullock Carts and Motor Bikes: Ancient India on a New Road by Beth Roy. Atheneum, New York, 1972, pages 143–147.

States. The federal government provides money in the form of grants-in-aid to the states and maintains several national universities. It attempts to coordinate educational programs throughout the country, offering advice, and assisting the states with textbooks, teachers and equipment.

Elementary Education.   There are over 55 million children between the ages of six and eleven in the primary grades. This is more than the number of American children of the same ages in school. In the United States, however, almost every child is in school; in India only two-thirds of the children of primary school age are in school.

The other third don't go to school because there is no school in their neighborhood or village. It is almost impossible to travel to the next village where there may be a school, because there is no transportation, perhaps not even a road. Some parents are too poor to send their children to school so they keep them at home to help in the work on the tiny farm or around the house. There may be no teacher available for the school they do have. School teachers are paid very low salaries; they do not command much respect in the community. Many teachers are unwilling to serve in rural areas far from cities where living conditions are so very poor. There are no recreational or home comforts and few opportunities for advancement.

Even today, only a third of the entering class in first grade will continue to go to school after four years. And the number of girls who attend school is much lower than that of boys— partly because parents in many rural areas feel that educating girls is a waste of time.

What is taught in these grades? The teacher, largely through the lecture method (for there are never enough books to go around) shows children how to read by writing each word on the blackboard and having children repeat it aloud. They then write the word on small slates or in the dust on the floor. In this way they are taught the elements of reading, writing, spelling, and arithmetic.

Gandhi recommended a program of basic education for these schools. He favored teaching the home skills and crafts—cooking, spinning, weaving, and carpentry—in addition to the basic subjects. In this way, he believed, children would be taught to take their places as productive members of the community. From the sale of the products made by the children, textbooks, notebooks and other materials could be purchased to help make the school a little self-supporting. The government sends teachers from its Community Development Program to carry out this Basic Education program which has been adopted in many schools.

Secondary Education. There are over 75,000 secondary schools with an enrollment of about 40 million students. Many of the schools are state-supported; others are private schools.

The course of study in the secondary schools is determined by university entrance examinations. That is, the subjects taught are mainly for the purpose of passing the examinations that will determine entrance to a university. Much of the instruction is in English, and this creates a serious problem for students whose native language is not English. They have to study English in addition to their regional language. Most textbooks are written in English. The regional languages do not have technical terms, particularly in the sciences and mathematics, thus limiting their use in instruction.

The final examinations are another problem; they are made up by teachers other than the classroom instructors. The exams are based on memorization of facts, and grades on these exams are all-important. The work done by students throughout the year does not count. Those students who pass go on to the next grade, or graduate and are accepted into university level programs. Those students who fail either repeat the subject or drop out of school. Almost half of the students fail their school finals.

University Education. In spite of the difficulty of the entrance examination, there has been a great increase in the number of students at the universities. In 1947 there were 200,000 students; in 1966 there were 1½ million. There are now over 45 universities and about 800 colleges with over 3.7 million students. All of these, except for four national universities, are under state control.

The language problem continues to be serious in the university. Most of the courses are taught in English; less than a quarter of the universities offer courses taught in Hindi or one of the regional languages. Many of the students who enter the university are not well trained in English. It is very difficult for them to use the English textbooks or to understand the professors' lectures in English. With examinations the determining factor in a student's grade the stress is on memorization rather than individual creative work. The low pay does not attract the best qualified professors.

The curriculum of the universities is mainly oriented toward the liberal arts. The humanities courses, such as literature, Greek and Latin, Western history and art, attract almost 70 per cent of the students. Yet India's great need is for trained engineers, scientists, doctors and technologists. Thousands of students want a college degree for the sake of the degree itself and not because of the type of training involved. Many are afraid of and unwilling to take a science course because of possible failure, so they take what they think is an easier course—the humanities. To use the university to train for a career runs counter to the traditional Indian belief that learning is an end in itself and should not be related to the mere earning of a living.

Since independence, the government has been putting greater stress on professional education. Technical colleges and polytechnical institutes have been opened, with an enrollment of over 185,000 students. The number of graduates in engineering and technology has increased greatly over the past thirty years. Fourteen rural universities stress vocational programs that include water-control engineering, scientific farming, and rural sociology.

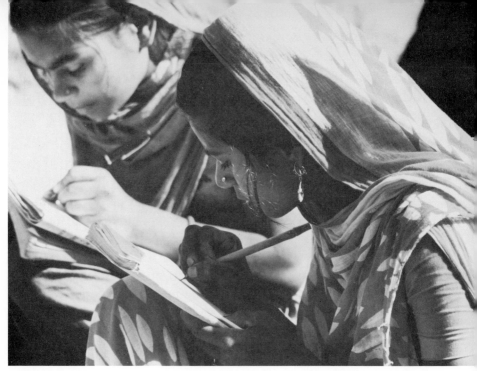

United Nations/C. Srinivasan

Two young mothers learning to write in a literacy class at a village near Lucknow. The Indian government also provides classes in family planning and health education.

Adult Education. There are over 200 million Indian adults who are illiterate. The states, with some assistance from the federal government, have set up over 50,000 adult groups called "social education classes" at which the basic elements of literacy are taught, plus lessons in citizenship, health, sanitation and training in elementary crafts such as sewing.

Achievements in Science. The Indian government, in the last 10 years, has developed a chain of more than 25 National Laboratories to conduct high-level research in applied science in a wide variety of fields from nuclear physics to solar energy. One institute is working on methods to use India's low-grade coal. A food research institute at Mysore is conducting experiments on new food products.

In 1968 the Bhabha Atomic Research Center near Bombay was opened, which will greatly increase the country's electric power and provide needed research in agricultural and medical applications of atomic energy.

The role of the intellectual is honored in India. A distinguished scientist, Dr. C. V. Raman, won the Nobel Prize in physics in 1930. Other scientists have won world-wide honors and fame. There are more than 250,000 highly educated people in India today, a figure surpassed in Asian countries only by Japan and China.

The contrast between the illiterate and the intellectual is enormous. The government is making a very serious effort to improve not only the quality (which is admittedly low) but also the quantity (which is already great, but not great enough) of education for its people.

The Role of Private Schools.   The best schools in India are private schools, such as St. Xavier's, run by Catholic religious orders. Many Indian leaders send their children to these schools.

E.   URBAN LIFE

About 120 million Indian people live in the cities. The rapid rate of growth of cities since independence has been due to the movement of people from the villages. Most of the Indian migrants left their villages because of overpopulation there and a lack of earning opportunities. Sons of farmers could not inherit parts of their fathers' land, already too small to provide a living. So they moved away to the city.

As part of the new Five Year Plan, the Indian government is promoting rural and cottage industrial development to encourage people to remain in the villages. This program is intended to solve some of the unemployment and urban problems in such overcrowded cities as Calcutta.

Of the 8.3 million people who live in Calcutta, more than 3 million live in miserable slum dwellings called *bustees*. Thousands of people sleep in the city's streets every night because they have no homes of their own. Cholera, spread by open

An American doctor examines children for smallpox. The disease had been considered virtually wiped out, but several new cases have been discovered in India.

sewers that often drain into the water system, is so widespread that the city has been called "the cholera capital of the world." Unemployment is serious. Transportation is almost impossible. The narrow streets, the crowded population, the scarcity of buses and cars, even of bicycles, make it a very congested city.

Government planners, using Calcutta as a model, are proposing to tear down the city slum tenements and build housing projects. Safe drinking water is to be provided, and underground sewers, paved streets, lighting and community bathhouses are to be constructed. Work projects to employ thousands are to be developed. Such a program costs money, a lot of money. In view of the limited funds available, it will take years to eliminate the intolerable features of city life.

F. THE ARTS OF INDIA

From ancient times almost all forms of classical art have been bound up in the spiritual life for the Hindu people. Architecture, music, the drama, painting—all reflect man's efforts to achieve union with God.

The Mogul rulers carried on this tradition with their beautiful mosques and tombs. They also introduced an art that portrayed the court and country life of contemporary people, animals and birds. The great architectural achievements of this period included the Agra Fort, the Taj Mahal, the Red Fort at Delhi, and Akbar's mausoleum at Sinkandra.

Since independence, modern Indian art has shown considerable growth with increased variations in styles: some based on old themes, others employing new ideas. The architectural design of the city of Chandigarh, the capital of Punjab, has received world attention. In these buildings, traditional Indian designs are skillfully blended with modern ones.

Indian dancing is also largely religious in concept. It was a highly developed at least 2,000 years ago. There are several important types of Indian dance. They include the *Bharata Natyam, Kathakali,* and *Kathak.* Bharata Natyam, the most famous, was born in the temples of the south, and is highly stylized. It takes over 10 years of intensive training to produce a dancer accomplished in the traditional gestures and footwork. There are some 140 distinct and recognized poses, and the dancer must show a remarkable control over his muscles, particularly those of the face, neck and hands.

Kathakali is an ancient dance-drama of Peral which is characterized by elaborate makeup, rich costumes and fantastic headdresses. The brilliantly dressed dancers take their themes from the great Indian epics. They use mime, which employs subtle facial expressions and elaborate hand movements.

The third dance type, called Kathak, is found largely in northern India. It interprets short episodes from the early life of Krishna and also the everyday life of the people. It features lightning footwork and requires an excellent sense of rhythm. There is also a wealth of material in the folk dances of India; the most famous is Manipuri, for which very beautiful and distinctive clothes are worn. Whatever the form of dancing, the art of pantomime, which is without sound, is highly developed. The dancer is, essentially, a story teller; therefore, each gesture of eye or eyebrow, hand or finger, neck or foot has its traditional unalterable meaning.

Indian music is not easy for an American to understand or appreciate. It is essentially melodic, not harmonic, and is based on a highly elaborate system of notes and melodies. Each piece of music consists of a particular arrangement of notes, called a *raga* (of which there are over 70,000), and is intended to portray a particular emotion or feeling, or create the flavor of a particular season or time. The music is played on stringed instruments, such as the *tambura* and *sitar;* on wind instruments, including flutes; and percussion instruments, such as drums, particularly the *mridanganda* and *tabla.*

Indian culture, as expressed through its art, music and dance, continues to reflect age-old traditions and customs, even under the impact of 20th-century European influences.

G.   THE ROLE OF WOMEN IN INDIA

During British Rule.   When the Muslims conquered and ruled a large part of India, they introduced the custom of *purdah*— the seclusion of women and the covering of their faces in the company of all except their immediate family. Other practices developed which indicated the inferior position of women: child marriages, polygamy, *suttee* (see page 69). Although the British abolished *suttee* and weakened other traditional practices, they permitted the personal laws of the various religious groups and castes to prevail in matters of marriage, inheritance of property and family relations. In villages, even today, women keep out of sight when men are present.

Before Independence. Under Gandhi's leadership women were encouraged to take an active part in his civil-disobedience campaigns. They picketed shops, prepared and distributed literature, and served as messengers.

Some of the Indian states permitted women to vote, provided they met property and educational requirements. Very few women could qualify. The Constitution of 1950 granted the right to vote to all adult men and women without property or educational requirements.

Since Independence. Although religious opposition from orthodox Hindus was strong, Nehru was able to have many laws adopted that changed the legal and social status of women. Polygamy is prohibited by law, and divorce is now recognized. Minimum ages for marriage were set at 15 for females and 18 for males. The rights of women to adopt children, to inherit property, to buy and sell and otherwise engage in activities closed before to them, have also been made into law.

Many new careers are opening for the modern woman. Medicine is one, politics another, teaching a third. Unfortunately, the ancient traditions that emphasize a wife's submission,

A female student at the India Institute of Technology suggests the progress India has made toward equality of the sexes.

United Nations

obedience, devotion and dedication to her husband's every wish still bind the Hindu woman in spite of her legal emancipation.

There are some outstanding women in public life. Nehru's sister, Mme. Pandit, served as Indian Ambassador to Moscow and to Washington and as the President of the United Nations General Assembly in 1953-54—the only woman elected to fill this office. Some universities have women chancellors, and many colleges have women principals. The present Prime Minister of India is a woman—Mme. Indira Gandhi, daughter of Nehru.

Such women are exceptions. The vast majority of women are far less educated than men. Emancipation has not yet brought equality to Indian women.

QUESTIONS AND ACTIVITIES

MULTIPLE CHOICE TEST

In each of the following you have three choices. Choose the only correct answer.

1. India's industrial development is limited by (*a*) lack of natural resources, (*b*) unwillingness of the government to support this program, (*c*) insufficient capital.
2. Much of the money to build industry in India comes from (*a*) foreign aid, (*b*) loans by Indians, (*c*) internal taxes.
3. The average annual income of an Indian today is about (*a*) $50, (*b*) $160, (*c*) $250.
4. India's rapid population increase has been made possible by (*a*) growth of wealth of the average family, (*b*) improvements in disease and sickness controls, (*c*) adequate food supplies for the country.
5. The most important single occupation of the Indian people is (*a*) factory work, (*b*) farming, (*c*) trade and commerce.
6. Which is not a problem of India? (*a*) overpopulation, (*b*) poverty, (*c*) agricultural surpluses.
7. Farmers in India (*a*) use new and complicated machinery, (*b*) are helped by large amounts of fertilizer, (*c*) generally have very small farms.

8. Farm productivity in India is (*a*) less than, (*b*) greater than, (*c*) equal to the average of Japanese and American farm productivity.

9. In trying to increase food production, India has emphasized (*a*) mass collectivization of farms, (*b*) reducing expenditures for irrigation projects, (*c*) the demonstration of new farming methods.

10. The changed position of women in Indian society is best illustrated by (*a*) the abolition of *purdah*, (*b*) the election of women to office, (*c*) the continued recognition of polygamy.

11. Education in India is largely controlled by (*a*) the individual states, (*b*) the central government, (*c*) the local villages.

12. The main language of instruction in Indian universities today is (*a*) Hindi, (*b*) English, (*c*) Bengali.

13. The course of study in India's secondary schools is determined by (*a*) the individual teacher, (*b*) university entrance examinations, (*c*) the national department of education.

14. India's efforts to increase food production and industrialization are being encouraged by (*a*) centralized planning, (*b*) the individual states, (*c*) local governments.

15. The first Five Year Plan of India concentrated on *(a)* development of industries, *(b)* construction of railroads, *(c)* increasing food production.

16. As a result of the first three Five Year Plans, food production in India (*a*) has increased so that the country is self-sufficient, (*b*) has not kept up with the rapid increase in population, (*c*) has been helped a great deal by the widespread use of modern machines.

17. The voluntary cooperation of the Indian peasant is being sought through the (*a*) Community Development Program, (*b*) appeals of religious leaders, (*c*) enlistment of foreign advisors.

18. *Panchayat* is an Indian term meaning (*a*) dressing gown, (*b*) breakfast food, (*c*) local council.

19. Much land in India was owned by (*a*) *zamindars*, (*b*) *gurus*, (*c*) *dhotis*.

20. Land reform in India has as its major purpose (*a*) the use of machinery, (*b*) the digging of wells, (*c*) the breakup of large estates and their distribution among the landless.

21. Irrigation projects are essential in (*a*) northwest India, (*b*) northeast India, (*c*) southwest India.

22. The Tata factories are India's chief (*a*) automobile plants, (*b*) steel mills, (*c*) bicycle works.

23. "Cottage industries" refer to (*a*) the production of steel, (*b*) the mining of coal, (*c*) the local production of textiles.

24. The Indian government owns and operates (*a*) all the industries in the country, (*b*) the railroads and airlines, (*c*) the factories making cotton cloth and automobiles.

25. India's electricity is used mainly (*a*) in the home, (*b*) on the railroads, (*c*) in industry.

26. The examination system used in India's secondary schools and colleges (*a*) tests memorization of facts, (*b*) does not prevent many students from graduating, (*c*) is made up by the teachers of the students.

27. About (*a*) 10 per cent, (*b*) 20 per cent, (*c*) 30 per cent of the Indian people are literate.

28. Indian villages (*a*) have many modern conveniences such as electricity and plumbing, (*b*) always have a school, (*c*) are small.

29. Many Indians left their farm homes to go to the city because they believed (*a*) there were better job opportunities in the city, (*b*) the city offered more adequate housing and comforts, (*c*) there was no future in the village.

30. The diet of the average Indian (*a*) is deficient in proteins and vitamins, (*b*) contains a large amount of beef, (*c*) helps to keep him in good general health.

KEY WORDS AND PHRASES

Can you explain the meaning or importance of the following words or phrases?

Gramdan
land reform
Community Development
  Program
"Land gift" movement
"cottage industries"
zamindars
centralized planning

gram sevak
standard of living
Basic Education
farm productivity
Five Year Plan
panchayat
Tata Works
Bhoodan

TRUE OR FALSE

Do you agree with the following statements? Give reasons for your answers.

1. Indian natural resources are inadequate to promote industrialism.
2. Indian agriculture is faced with many problems.
3. The rapid increase of population in India is typical of other underdeveloped countries.
4. The Five Year Plans of India are similar in purpose and accomplishments to the Soviet Union's Five Year Plans.
5. The Community Development Program is an example of democratic planning on a local scale.
6. There has been an increase in the number of peasant land owners in India since independence.
7. India raises enough food to feed its people.
8. Sons are more desired than daughters by Indian families.
9. World War II stimulated the creation and growth of Indian industries.
10. Cottage industries employ more workers than the steel, automobile and shoe industries.
11. India is as socialist as the Soviet Union is.
12. American aid has helped all Indian industries grow.
13. India has very little water potential for electricity.
14. Indian education today is still dominated by programs and policies inherited from the British.
15. Women in India are still hidden behind "the veil."

COMPLETION TEST

For each of the following statements add the word MOST, SOME, or FEW that would make each statement correct.

1. .... Indians live in villages.
2. .... Indian students go on to and graduate from the university.
3. .... Indians have an adequate diet.
4. .... industries are owned and operated by the Indian government.
5. .... Indians eat meat as part of their diet.

6. .... Indians believe in the Hindu religion.

7. .... Indians speak English.

8. .... Indians suffer from at least one serious disease in their lives.

9. .... Indian states have a college or university of their own.

10. .... Indians are farmers.

THINGS TO DO

1. Prepare a class report on the current Indian Five Year Plan. Consult the *Reader's Guide to Periodical Literature* for articles. Include in your report: purposes, programs, financing, and results.

2. Make a graph showing Indian agricultural and industrial production as compared to that of the United States and Communist China. Consult an almanac for this information.

3. Draw a resource map of India, locating major natural resources, industrial centers, and irrigation projects.

4. Create a cartoon illustrating the Indian farmer's problems.

5. Write a newspaper article about "Village Life in India."

6. Prepare a class report comparing your school system and classes with those of India students. Include in your report, the subjects taught, the language of instruction, textbooks and materials used, the numbers of students attending schools. Consult the card catalogue of your school or public library for information.

7. Divide the class into committees, each of which should report on one of the following topics: American Food Aid to India; Indian and Soviet Socialism Compared; the Tata Steel Works; Irrigation Projects and Their Importance; Gandhi's Basic Education Program.

8. Write an outline for a newspaper or magazine story on the problems of overcrowding in India's major cities. Include information on housing, employment opportunities, business and industry, and crime. Make suggestions for illustrations to complement your story.

9. Consult the *Encyclopaedia Britannica* or any other encyclopedia and write a composition on "Purdah." Follow this up with a class report on "The Hindu Woman Today."

INDIA IN THE WORLD OF NATIONS

7

A. POLICY OF NON-ALIGNMENT

India is often regarded as the spokesperson for the developing third world nations. In fact, since India became independent it has played a major role in international as well as Asian affairs. This is not surprising. India's size and large population alone make its voice strong and significant. Its vast resources and industrial progress make India the second leading industrialized nation in Asia. And the peaceful way in which India secured its freedom, led by such figures as Gandhi and Nehru, became a model for other countries under foreign control. India's long history, and the many diplomatic ties with Western nations before 1947 has shaped its course of foreign involvement. A course which is still followed today—a policy of *non-alignment.*

Many leaders of the Western world labelled India's policy as "neutral." Nehru denied this very bitterly. A neutral country, he said, will not intervene on either side of a dispute, no matter what the cause. He referred to his policy as "non-alignment," under which a nation decides each question involving other countries on its own merits, and reserves freedom to take what steps it feels will help to resolve the conflict. He argued that such a policy would check the growing division of the world into two opposing camps. It would limit possible violence by enabling India to serve as a mediator, one with no axe of its own to grind, and thus help the cause of peace. This policy became very popular with many of the new, small and weak nations who were reluctant to choose sides in the Cold War. India became their leader.

The non-alignment policy of Nehru was not understood by many Americans. They could not grasp the seemingly contradictory Indian policies of accepting so much economic aid from the United States, yet opposing many measures favored by the United States. India persistently voted for Communist China's admission to the United Nations, and refused to support the American resolution condemning Soviet aggression in Hungary and Czechoslovakia. They heard Nehru condemn the use of aggression, yet they watched India seize the Portuguese enclave of Goa.

B. FOREIGN COLONIES IN INDIA

When Britain granted independence to India in 1947, France and Portugal still retained small holdings—a few ports on the subcontinent. Nehru called these "pimples on the face of India." They were constant reminders of Western imperialism. To free these colonies, or enclaves, seemed to be necessary if the Indians were to eliminate all evidences of Western control.

The French in India. Even though the French had been defeated by the British in their efforts to expand their control over India (see page 66) they continued to hold the ports of Pondichéry, Chandernagor, and several others. This French territory amounted to less than 200 square miles, with a population of some 350,000. In 1954, France voluntarily withdrew.

The Portuguese in India. The Portuguese were not so obliging. They held several tiny slices—Goa, Damão, and Diu on the west coast, and they had been there for over 450 years. They regarded these territories as "overseas provinces," and refused to withdraw. Although Nehru insisted that Goa must become part of India, he was opposed to the use of force to take it.

But suddenly, in December 1961, the Indian army invaded Goa and took it over. In spite of American and United Nations efforts to prevent this use of force, the Indian government occupied the other Portuguese possessions and thus eliminated the last foreign holdings in the country.

During the 18th and 19th centuries, the native princes who ruled India (above) were too divided to oppose successfully the well-armed, highly organized British army (below).

C. RELATIONS WITH PAKISTAN

Partition of India in 1947 into the two Muslim states of Pakistan and Hindu India intensified many old problems and created new ones. What had been political, religious and economic rivalries between two groups of people in the same country became international incidents involving two independent states. Even the division of money, factory and office equipment, railroad cars and river waters became international problems. The rioting and killing that accompanied the mass migrations of Hindus and Muslims from one state to the other made the already bad feelings worse.

The Indus River System Problem.   The Indus River flows through Pakistan. During British occupation, an extensive system of irrigation canals had been built to provide the necessary water for the farmlands of that province. However, the Indus River also flows through India. When Pakistan became independent, the Muslim government was afraid that India would divert the waters of the Indus River and some of its tributaries for its own use, thus turning much of Pakistan's irrigated land into desert.

This problem was taken up by the International Bank for Reconstruction and Development, an agency of the United Nations, which secured an agreement in 1960 that was satisfactory to both countries. Under this agreement, the waters of three western rivers (the Indus, the Jhelum and the Chenab) are reserved for Pakistan's use, and the waters of three eastern rivers (the Ravi, the Beas, and the Sutlej) for Indian use. Since two-thirds of the irrigated area and 40 million Pakistani (as against 10 million Indians) are dependent upon these rivers for irrigation, the division gave Pakistan the greater amount of water.

New dams, reservoirs and irrigation works are being constructed by both countries to increase by 30 million acres the cultivated areas in the northwest. This billion-dollar program is being helped by contributions from the United States, the World Bank, and other countries.

Kashmir. Kashmir in northwestern India was the largest princely state before partition. Its population of over 5 million lives in an area of 85,000 square miles. The ruler of Kashmir is a Hindu *maharajah* but about three-fourths of the population are Muslims. When India was divided in 1947, the *maharajah* was given the choice of joining with either Pakistan or India.

While he was deciding, Muslim tribesmen from Pakistan invaded Kashmir. This persuaded the Hindu ruler to join India. Indian troops were quickly sent into Kashmir. Pakistan sent in its soldiers. India appealed to the United Nations which succeeded, after a year of fighting, in arranging a cease-fire in January 1949. The western and northern parts of the disputed territory (about one-third of its total area) were in Pakistani hands; the remaining two-thirds under Indian control.

Under the cease-fire agreement, provision was made for a plebiscite to allow the people of Kashmir to choose for themselves which country they want to join. The United Nations was to hold this plebiscite. This has never been done, in spite of United Nations efforts to secure Pakistani-Indian cooperation.

The Indian government introduced economic and social reforms in the Kashmir area it held in an effort to persuade the people to become part of India. In 1957 India incorporated its Kashmir territory. Pakistan objected, and tried again to get the United Nations to hold the promised plebiscite.

The strategic location of Kashmir and the announced government policy of equality for all religions strengthened Indian determination to keep Kashmir.

In 1962, China attacked India and took over some 12,000 miles of Indian territory. In 1963, Pakistan reached an agreement with China regarding the borders of Pakistan-held Kashmir. The drawing together of Pakistan and China caused India many misgivings. Relations between Pakistan and India grew worse.

Border violation charges increased between India and Pakistan in 1965. Sharp fighting broke out near the southern Pakistani-Indian border. This was halted by a cease-fire within a month. In September 1965, a full-fledged war involving planes, tanks

MAP OF KASHMIR

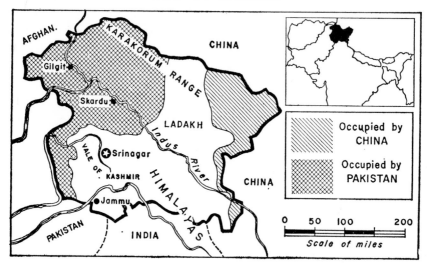

and soldiers, broke out between the two countries, as each invaded the other's territory. For three weeks, this undeclared war went on. Then the United Nations Security Council succeeded in securing a cease-fire agreement.

In January 1966, the Soviet Union brought the leaders of the two countries together—Shastri of India and Ayub Khan of Pakistan—at Tashkent, in the U.S.S.R., to discuss their differences. Out of the conference came an agreement by the two countries to withdraw their soldiers to positions held before the fighting.

After the Indian-Pakistani war in 1971 that resulted in the creation of an independent Bangladesh from the former state of East Pakistan (see Chapter 8), new meetings were held on the Kashmir issue. In July 1972, Pakistani President Ali Bhutto and Indian Prime Minister Gandhi, signed a peace treaty. Later, a joint statement was issued which laid down guidelines for demarcation of the disputed Kashmir border and said it would be "respected by both sides without prejudice to the recognized positions of either side."

Although Kashmir remains partitioned, India and Pakistan have begun to resume diplomatic and economic ties. In November 1974, the two governments signed a treaty reestablishing trade relations. Diplomatic ties as well as air and rail service were resumed in July 1976. The two nations continue to assess each other's moves cautiously, especially nuclear weapon research and defense spending and development.

D. RELATIONS WITH THE SOVIET UNION

Although India has continued to maintain its foreign policy based on non-alignment in order to encourage friendly and peaceful relations among all nations, government officials have built a close relationship with the Soviet Union. Since 1971, when India and the U.S.S.R. signed a mutual peace treaty, the two nations have enjoyed strong diplomatic ties.

Relations between India and the Soviet Union have been very good for a number of reasons:

1. Geographically the two countries, although not next-door neighbors, are very close to each other. The southern part of Asiatic Russia is separated from Kashmir by a very thin strip of Afghanistan territory.

2. Ideologically, there is much similarity between the two countries. India's efforts to improve its industrial and agricultural output through centrally-planned Five Year Plans are similar to the Soviet Union's economic program. Government control of large sectors of the economy is strikingly similar in both countries. The economic progress made by the U.S.S.R. in the last 40 years is an inspiration to the Indian leaders who hope to do for their country what the Soviet leaders have done for theirs. Although the Communist Party is not very large in India, it has grown steadily since 1947.

3. Diplomatically, the two countries have been friendly since 1947. Soviet leaders, like Khrushchev and Kosygin, paid state visits to India, and Indian leaders have visited Moscow. The U.S.S.R. supported India's actions in Goa and Kashmir. The Soviet Union supplied late-model planes when China attacked in 1962, and offered to build factories in India so that India could make its own planes. It was Soviet diplomacy that brought Indian and Pakistani leaders together at Tashkent in 1966 to agree to withdraw their troops from each other's territory.

4. Economically, the Soviet Union has been of great financial and technical help to India. The U.S.S.R. has loaned India over one billion dollars in the past twenty-five years, most of its going to build oil refineries and steel plants. Soviet technicians have been training Indian workers to operate these new factories. Soviet food shipments have enabled India to overcome wheat shortages. This aid has been widely publicized in India and has created a very favorable image of the U.S.S.R.

Soviet-Indian relations improved in 1968, beginning with a visit to India by Premier Kosygin. The visit resulted in agreements on trade, defense and weapon sales, cultural and educational exchanges, and increased Soviet loans.

5. A twenty-year treaty of peace, friendship, and cooperation was signed between India and the U.S.S.R. in 1971. The Soviet Union launched an Indian-built satellite into orbit in 1975, and this event was followed by an official state visit to Moscow by Prime Minister Gandhi. Relations continue to improve and strengthen between the two nations.

E. RELATIONS WITH COMMUNIST CHINA

India's problems with Communist China in the past rank second only to its difficulties with Pakistan. When China occupied Tibet in 1950, it became India's next-door neighbor. Relations between the two countries were friendly until 1962.

India was one of the strongest supporters of Red China's admission to the United Nations. Over the years, exchanges of official visits of leaders, of agricultural and technical experts, and cultural delegations, had brought the two countries close together. Both countries were breaking away from foreign controls. Both were pursuing programs to improve the standard of living of their people.

Nehru and Mao Tse-tung of China, in 1954, agreed on a general statement of principles, which Nehru called the *Panch Shila.* Its "five principles" included mutual non-aggression, respect for territorial integrity, non-interference in domestic affairs, peaceful coexistence and equality. These principles were reaffirmed the following year at the Bandung Conference of Afro-Asian nations, to which India had invited China.

Tibetan Revolt of 1959. The first major break between Red China and India took place when the people of Tibet revolted against the Chinese. This had been building up since the Chinese takeover in 1950. The religious ruler of the Tibetans—the Dalai Lama—was forced to flee into India where he was welcomed. Chinese troops thereupon crossed the eastern section of India's long northern border and occupied some Indian territory.

Nehru appealed to China to withdraw the soldiers and live up to the *Panch Shila* agreement. China countered by charging that the Indian government had encouraged the Tibetans to revolt, and demanded some 50,000 square miles of Indian territory that it claimed as Chinese. For the next three years, one country leveled charges against the other.

The Chinese Attack India. Suddenly, in October 1962, Chinese troops crossed the disputed boundary line between Tibet and India and defeated the Indian army stationed there. India appealed to both Britain and the United States for military help. Both countries rushed supplies. The United States sent small arms and ammunition and some transport planes to airlift Indian troops into the battle areas. Although Nehru also asked Russia for help, the Soviet government urged India to accept the Chinese proposal for a cease-fire, and delayed any military aid.

Just as quickly as it began, the fighting ended. The Chinese halted their attack, pulled their troops back, but kept much of the territory they had won. China still occupies the land it gained, and has declared that it is now Chinese territory.

Effects of the Invasion. One major result of this brief but sharp invasion was that India began to build up its armaments and defense positions. This meant that money and materials badly needed for the economic and social development of the country had to be diverted to military, not domestic purposes.

Many Indians took another look at Nehru's foreign policy of non-alignment. Questions were raised about the country's lack of military preparedness. The invasion created many doubts about India's leadership among the neutral nations of the world. Above all, it pointed up the deep rivalry between India and China, with the leadership of Asia hanging in the balance. To what extent would the smaller Asiatic nations and the neighbors of India—Bhutan and Nepal—be able to depend upon India in the event of trouble?

Another factor that had weakened Indian-Chinese relations was the threat of China as an atomic power. China had joined the atomic club by exploding atomic and hydrogen bombs. India also has the potential to become a nuclear power, and continues to devote research and financial resources in the peaceful as well as military applications of atomic energy.

Relations with China continued to deteriorate during the early 1970's, particularly as a result of China's support of Pakistan in the Pakistani civil war that resulted in the formation of Bangladesh. Tensions began to ease in 1976 when the two countries exchanged diplomatic representatives. Two years later, China sent a special trade delegation to India—the first such mission since 1962. Full diplomatic and economic relations are not yet realized, however, both countries seem determined to build closer ties for the future.

F.   INDIA AND THE UNITED STATES

The largest democracy in Asia and the largest democracy in the West have not always been the best of friends. Sympathy for Indian hopes of independence had been expressed by many Americans before and during World War II. After freedom had been achieved, the United States supported Indian admission into the United Nations, and hoped it would be a model for other new states to follow.

Conflicting American Opinions. The U.S. has found it somewhat difficult to support some of India's policies. The American government regards India as an important ally which if stable and viable would have a major influence on maintaining the peace and stability of Asia. Certainly the different geographic locations and different historical and cultural experiences require that patience prevail in working out a good relationship.

The American government has been concerned and confused that in the midst of severe economic difficulties the Indian government has devoted so much money, time, and resources to the development of a nuclear weapon. The Indian government still maintains its policy of nonalignment but claims that its status as a nuclear power will aid in bringing peace and stability to the world.

The ending of the state of emergency in 1977 relieved many Americans who were concerned with the disregard of human rights in India. During the late 1970's the United States government has been attempting, with success, to improve relations between the two nations.

Conflicting Indian Opinions. The Indians cannot understand why the United States has been building up Pakistan as a military ally. The Indians regard this as a threat to them, and them only. The formation of S.E.A.T.O. and the Bagdad Pact—anti-Communist alliances which Pakistan joined—are considered more dangerous to India than to the U.S.S.R. or China.

When the United States withdrew financial support for the building of a government-owned steel plant, the Indians regarded it as attempted interference with their form of government, and turned to the Soviets for help. When the United States offered to establish an Indo-American Foundation in India to promote progress in all fields of learning, Mme. Gandhi was forced to turn it down because of fear that it would be a cover for spy activities.

The American food aid program, while of tremendous help to the Indian people, is regarded with a great deal of suspicion; it is feared that it will be used to influence government policy toward the United States.

CASE INQUIRY: India's Foreign Policy

The following selection is an excerpt from an interview with former Prime Minister Moraji Desai in 1978.

> **Q Mr. Prime Minister, since you succeeded Indira Gandhi in 1977, have you shifted India's foreign relations away from the Soviet Union and toward the West?**
>
> **A** I am not pro-Western, nor pro-Eastern, not pro-anybody. I am pro-everybody. Why should I be pro-anybody?
>
> That is what I made clear to them in Moscow, and also to Mr. Carter when he was here in January. We are equally friends to all. Friendship with you should not be at the cost of friendship with someone else. I think this is now understood in Moscow as well as in Washington. . . .
>
> **Q Are you interested in buying military equipment from Western nations instead of almost exclusively from the Soviet Union?**
>
> **A** We are interested in getting what we need wherever we can get it. We do not want to be discriminating in that.
>
> But if we buy more from Soviet Russia—as was done in the past—it is the fault of the Western countries. They did not sell to us. On the contrary, they helped those who were attacking us.
>
> **Q Do you share the criticism of some Asian leaders that the Carter administration puts too much emphasis on Europe and not enough on Asia and the Pacific region?**
>
> **A** I have never complained. I do not agree the United States is not interested in the countries of Asia. I am just as happy if there is not always too much attention paid to us—because you have to ask what kind of attention it is. . . .
>
> **Q What role do you foresee foreign investment playing in India's economic development?**
>
> **A** We welcome foreign investment in areas where we do not have technology and skills required. But in areas where we already have sufficient skills, then we do not want or need foreign investment.
>
> Where we lack technology, we must learn from others. In petroleum development, for example, we are taking technological help from France, America, Russia—everywhere. But we must learn and then be independent again, not remain perpetually dependent on someone else. That is the policy we follow.

1. According to Prime Minister Desai, what is the basic direction of Indian foreign policy?

2. How would you assess India's position on foreign investment?

"What India Wants Now from U.S.: Interview with Prime Minister Moraji Desai." *U.S. News and World Report,* vol. 84, June 19, 1978, pages 30–33.

American Aid to India. The United States has provided food and economic assistance to India since its independence. American technical aid has enabled India to build factories, train workers, construct dams and irrigation projects, and extend health programs. In addition, various American relief organizations and foundations have made large contributions to educational programs.

American economic aid was reduced in 1968. There were major differences between the U.S. and India on such issues as: India's stand against American involvement in Vietnam; India's silent support of the Soviet invasion of Czechoslovakia; and Indian-Soviet arms agreements and defense treaties.

The 1970's. Relations between the United States and India were seriously damaged by American support of Pakistan in 1971. Tensions eased somewhat in 1973, but flared again when the American government resumed military aid to Pakistan in 1975. The American government also harshly criticized India's suspension of civil liberties and widespread political repression under Prime Minister Gandhi.

In the past few years diplomatic and economic ties have been strengthened. President Carter visited India in 1978. Increased aid for industrial development and health care has also brought the two nations closer together.

G. INDIA'S NEIGHBORS—NEPAL AND BHUTAN

At the center of India's northern frontier, there is a stretch of about 1000 miles where India and China are separated by the countries of Nepal and Bhutan.

Nepal. This is the larger of the two states; its area is about 54,000 square miles, and its population over 12 million. It is a constitutional monarchy, ruled by King Birenda. Nepal is a poor country, with more than 90 per cent illiteracy. It is important, however, as a stepping stone to the Indian subcontinent. The Nepalese are very proud of their independence, and have fought in the past to keep it. Their warrior class—the Gurkhas—are excellent soldiers and many are serving in the Indian army today.

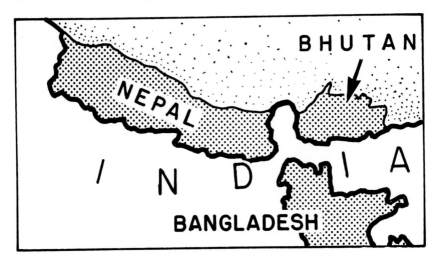

The Buddhist and Hindu religions are practiced in the country; tribal and caste distinctions are still observed. The lack of transportation and communication lines has hindered the industrial development of this small nation.

India realizes the importance of this country and has maintained good relations by a substantial aid program for road building, irrigation projects, drinking water purification and power projects. The United States also contributes assistance to Nepal, as do Britain, the Soviet Union and China. Much of this aid is for the construction of an east-west road which will link areas of the country that can be reached only by traveling through India.

Bhutan. This semi-independent kingdom between India and Tibet has an area of about 18,000 miles and a population of 1.4 million. Although the kingdom has its own ruler, the *Druk Gyalpo* (Dragon King), its defense and foreign relations are directed by India. Bhutan's people are ethnically related to the Tibetans. Buddhism is the dominant religion. In recent years Bhutan has been evolving into a "democratic monarchy" in which the national assembly has veto power over the king.

QUESTIONS AND ACTIVITIES

MULTIPLE CHOICE TEST

In each of the following you have three choices. Choose the only correct answer.

1. Under Nehru's leadership, India began a policy of (*a*) alliances with Western states, (*b*) alliances with the Soviet Union, (*c*) non-alignment.

2. India has consistently (*a*) voted for the admission of Communist China to the United Nations, (*b*) favored a policy of cooperation with Communist China, (*c*) took no stand on China.

3. The chief conflict between Pakistan and India has been over (*a*) the boundaries of Pakistan, (*b*) Kashmir, (*c*) Goa.

4. French ports in India were (*a*) seized by force, (*b*) given up through United Nations intervention, (*c*) ceded by mutual agreement.

5. India secured Goa by (*a*) force, (*b*) diplomatic agreement, (*c*) a decision of the World Court.

6. Goa was a colony of (*a*) France, (*b*) Britain, (*c*) Portugal.

7. The great majority of the people in Kashmir are '(*a*) Muslims, (*b*) Hindus, (*c*) Bengalis.

8. A plebiscite is a (*a*) law passed by the Indian legislature, (*b*) yes or no vote, (*c*) decision by the United Nations.

9. Soviet help to India has been of great value in (*a*) containing India's population growth, (*b*) developing transportation facilities, (*c*) building up the Indian steel industry.

10. The Kashmir dispute (*a*) has been settled, (*b*) has not been settled, (*c*) is being settled by the United Nations.

11. India is (*a*) a member of the United Nations, (*b*) belongs to the Southeast Asia Treaty Organization, (*c*) has refused to join the United Nations.

12. Under the Indus River Agreement (*a*) India received the greater share of its waters, (*b*) Pakistan received the greater share of its waters, (*c*) both countries received equal amounts of the waters.

13. A cease-fire agreement in the India-Pakistan war of 1965 was brought about by (*a*) the United States, (*b*) SEATO, (*c*) the United Nations Security Council.

14. India is (*a*) unwilling to receive any foreign aid, (*b*) willing to be given foreign aid from any source, (*c*) able to finance its own economic growth.

15. The Chinese attack on India in 1962 was due to (*a*) India's aggressive attitude over Kashmir, (*b*) India's claims to territory on the northeast frontier, (*c*) India's support of America's foreign policies.

16. Following the 1977 elections and the victory of the Janata Party, the new Prime Minister became (*a*) Lal Shastri, (*b*) Moraji Desai, (*c*) Charan Singh.

17. The largest democracy in Asia is (*a*) Indonesia, (*b*) China, (*c*) India.

18. An important reason for India's misunderstanding of American policies has been due to (*a*) America's military aid to Pakistan, (*b*) American support of an atomic test ban treaty, (*c*) America's unwillingness to help India build up its atomic weapons.

19. Most of American aid to India has been in (*a*) military assistance, (*b*) food shipments, (*c*) industrial equipment.

20. American economic aid to India has been (*a*) greater than, (*b*) equal to, (*c*) less than Russian aid to India.

21. Although relations between India and Pakistan were gradually improving during the 1970's, Pakistan became concerned over (*a*) India's continued support of China, (*b*) India's explosion of an atomic device in 1974, (*c*) India's friendship with the United States.

22. The Gurkhas are well known for their (*a*) literary achievements, (*b*) artistic accomplishments, (*c*) fighting abilities.

23. Both of India's northern neighbors are (*a*) strong military states, (*b*) have their own rulers, (*c*) Buddhist in religion.

24. Kashmir is valuable because of its (*a*) strategic location, (*b*) important natural resources, (*c*) great natural beauty.

25. India is of great concern to the people of the United States because (*a*) of its military strength, (*b*) it is the largest democratic state in Asia, (*c*) it has great supplies of rubber, tin and oil.

KEY WORDS OR PHRASES

Can you explain the meaning and importance of the following words or phrases?

non-alignment	Indus River Agreement
enclave	Gurkha
Panch Shila	Tashkent Conference
cease-fire agreement	Dalai Lama
neutralism	Kashmir plebiscite

TRUE OR FALSE

Do you agree or disagree with the following statements? Give reasons for your answers.

1. "Neutralism and non-alignment are not the same policies," said Nehru.
2. India has been attacked but has never attacked other countries since it gained independence.
3. India is the largest democratic state in Asia.
4. American aid to India has been more economic than military.
5. The Indus River Agreement is of mutual benefit to both Pakistan and India.
6. Portugal and France reached peaceful understanding with India over their possessions in that country.
7. The United Nations has been successful in negotiating a solution of the Kashmir problem.
8. India is a strong atomic power.
9. India, Communist China and the Soviet Union have identical economic systems.
10. The United States supports India's efforts toward economic growth and development.

FACT OR OPINION

Which of the following statements are FACT and which are merely someone's OPINION?

1. Nehru was the foreign minister of India for fifteen years.
2. The acquisition of Goa by India was accomplished by peaceful means.
3. India has attempted to build friendly relations with both the Soviet Union and the United States.

4. Some of the problems facing India today have existed for hundreds of years.
5. India supported Communist China's admission to the United Nations.
6. American food gifts have been larger than any other country's help to India.
7. The policy of non-alignment is the best one for India to follow.
8. The Tashkent Conference of 1966 helped improve relations between the Soviet Union and India.

THINGS TO DO

1. Prepare a bulletin board display on "American Aid to India." Include in it pictures and articles showing the variety and types of this assistance.
2. Draw a map of Kashmir, showing (*a*) its strategic importance, (*b*) its chief cities, (*c*) its natural resources and (*d*) the areas held by Pakistan and India.
3. Write a story for the class newspaper on "The Kashmir Dispute." Include in it the background of the dispute, the efforts at settlement, and its present status.
4. Prepare a debate on the topic: "The United States should increase its food shipments to India."
5. Using *The New York Times Index* and the *Readers Guide to Periodical Literature*, research news articles on India's foreign affairs with the United States, China, and the Soviet Union over the past two years.
6. Investigate and summarize the voting record of India in the United Nations.
7. Organize a committee to interview a person in your community who has travelled or lived in India. Before you interview this person, discuss with your classmates what questions you should ask. Draw up a report of such an interview.
8. Prepare a radio broadcast for the Indian people on "Radio Free Asia," informing them about the purposes and extent of American economic aid.
9. Use an opaque projector to show pictures to the class about India's relations with its neighbors. Use such sources as *Asia, Life,* and the *National Geographic* magazines.
10. Prepare a report on a book discussing India's relations with the United States.

PAKISTAN AND BANGLADESH

8

Until 1947 no one in the world had ever heard of Pakistan. Until 1971, Bangladesh (meaning "Bengal nation") was not even a word, the nation was known as East Pakistan. Yet today, both Pakistan and Bangladesh are nations. These two countries share in the history and civilizations that shaped the development of India and were also part of the British empire of colonies from the eighteenth to the twentieth century. But there are many important differences between India and the nations of Pakistan and Bangladesh.

We have already read about the history of India and the struggle for independence in preceding chapters. What happened to India in 1947 following the second World War is now history; yet that history is constantly being repeated in the continuing shifting of political borders and the ever-changing alignments because of religious sentiment and strong nationalistic feelings. In spite of a common historic background, nourished over many centuries, the differences in geographic, religious, and economic basics finally resulted in the splitting of the subcontinent of India into the three separate nations that exist there today.

In this chapter we will examine the history of the partition of Pakistan following World War II and the civil war which led to the division of Pakistan into two separate nations—Pakistan and Bangladesh.

A. BACKGROUND TO PAKISTANI INDEPENDENCE

Long before the arrival of the British in India, and long before the coming of the Muslims, the Hindu influence had held sway for many centuries. The influence of Islam on the subcontinent of India began in the eighth century when Arabs from the Middle East first settled in the Indus River region. Several hundred years later, Muslims from Central Asia poured in through the Khyber Pass. The social order of Islam, based on the principle of human equality and universal brotherhood, greatly influenced the caste-dominated Hindu society. By the seventeenth century, almost the entire subcontinent was under the rule of the Mogul Empire. In time, the empire began to fall apart because of internal rivalry and European colonization and domination.

The Mogul Empire ended in 1857, and the struggle for independence began. The Muslims gradually lost their political power and social prestige. They were overshadowed by the overwhelming Hindu majority and the colonial policies of the European nations in Asia, particularly the British. The political re-awakening of the Muslims began with the efforts of Sir Said Ahmad Khan to revive their political and social rights. The result was the creation of the All-India Muslim League in 1906.

For a while Muslims cooperated with Hindus in the movement for Indian independence. Two great leaders changed the course of history for India's millions of Muslims. One was Muhammad Iqbal, who through his poetry exalted the Islamic cultural heritage and stressed patriotism. Before his death in 1938, he had popularized the idea of a single, independent Muslim state in India. The man who made this a reality was Muhammad Ali Jinnah.

Muhammad Ali Jinnah. Born in Karachi in 1876, he received an English education, studied law, entered politics as a supporter of the Indian Congress party, and advocated Hindu-Muslim cooperation. In 1920 he parted company with the Congress party because of its policy of non-cooperation with the British. He became president of the Muslim League and worked with Muhammad Iqbal for a separate Muslim state—Pakistan. The name of this state, it is said, came from P (Punjab), A (Afghan Province), K (Kashmir), S (Sind), (Baluchis-) TAN.

Another story is that its name means "land of the pure," and reflects the spiritual unity of its Muslim inhabitants.

Ali Jinnah's stubborn refusal to accept anything but a separate state for his people left the British no alternative but to yield to his demands. Therefore, when independence was granted to India in 1947, Pakistan was created as a dominion within the British Commonwealth. Ali Jinnah became its governor-general and the president of the Constituent Assembly, created to draw up a constitution for the new state.

The Problems of Partition. Unfortunately for Pakistan, Ali Jinnah died a year later. Liaquat Ali Khan became prime minister. The new leader faced many serious problems caused by the continued bad feelings between India and his country. Among these were the Kashmir question (still unresolved); control of the major rivers (particularly the Indus) which flow into Pakistan; the fact that Pakistan was split into eastern and western segments separated by almost 1,000 miles of India; and, as a result of the partition based almost solely upon religion, the largest migration of peoples the world has ever known.

Before this wholesale migration had ended, over 15 million people had moved—Muslims to Pakistan and Hindus to India. About nine million refugees went to India and some six million to Pakistan. It is estimated that more than half a million people died on this journey. There were many disputes over the property the refugees had left behind them, and the problems of settling and integrating these displaced millions were enormous. The leaders of Pakistan were hindered by a lack of administrative personnel and economic poverty of the country. The major industrial centers and the bulk of administrative machinery had remained in India.

Most of the trained officials in government service—whether in education, finance, or trade—were Indians. The raw materials were raised in the Muslim areas, but the processing factories for jute, the sugar refineries, and the spinning and weaving mills were in Indian hands. Thus, the producing areas were separated from the markets by partition. Even the division between the two countries of the physical assets of the old united country involved serious difficulties. How many locomotives, how many inkstands, how many typewriters, how much gold, how much of everything was to go to Pakistan? How much to India? Since India had the greater population, it received the larger share of almost everything. This only increased the bitterness between the two nations.

B. THE GOVERNMENT OF PAKISTAN

Following the death of Ali Jinnah in 1948, the National Assembly, acting under the amended British Dominion Act of 1935, elected Iskandar Mirza as acting governor-general. However, continued differences between East and West Pakistan delayed the framing of a new constitution. Finally, in early 1956, the differences were sufficiently overcome to permit the drawing up of a new constitution. Mirza was appointed provisional president and a republic was proclaimed.

Even the adoption of a new constitution did not settle the many problems facing the new country. The politicians were ambitious and greedy, various sections wanted to secede or obtain greater autonomy. Taxation was increased, graft and corruption spread and there was a general breakdown of law and order.

The 1958 Revolution. Continued unrest and cultural differences between West and East Pakistan caused a serious revolution in 1958. Martial law was declared and, in a coup, Field Marshal Ayub Khan replaced Mirza as president. In an election in 1960 Khan was confirmed as president and was reelected to a five-year term in 1965.

Under Ayub Khan's first administration, Pakistan enjoyed

a relatively stable government and seemed to be making some cultural, economic, and political progress. Martial law was ended in June, 1962, with the drafting of a new constitution providing for a stronger presidency.

After taking office in 1958, President Khan said, "Our ultimate aim is to restore democracy, but of the kind that people can understand and make work." He introduced what he called "Basic Democracies." This is a system of local self-government which begins at the village level. Several villages are grouped together into a Union Council; these councils are then joined into sub-district councils which are joined into District Councils, with Division Councils at the top.

Each of these four levels of the "Basic Democracies" represents a population unit of 1,000 people. Each of the 12,000 basic units has 10 elected members. Thus, each member is chosen by about 1,000 of his immediate neighbors. These 120,000 members make up the Electoral College of Pakistan. They elect the president, the members of the National Assembly, and the provincial legislatures.

The local Union Councils are in charge of agricultural, industrial and community development. They plan and construct roads, wells, irrigation canals, schools and clinics. The money for these programs comes from taxes, rates, tolls, and fees that the Union Council levies, in addition to contributions from the central government.

Under the New Constitution. A new constitution went into effect in 1962, providing for a president, a central legislature called the National Assembly, and a legislature with a governor in each province. The term of the president, and the legislature is five years, and all are elected by the "Basic Democracies."

During his term as president, Ayub Khan established order in the country and drew up a program for Pakistan's economic growth. Refugees were moved out of cities and resettled in the countryside; the educational system was expanded; land reform was adopted; agricultural production and industrial growth were stimulated.

Revolt in East Pakistan. One of the major problems Ayub Khan had to face, in spite of the many examples of progress he could point to, was the strong movement for greater autonomy in East Pakistan. Not long after he was reelected in 1965 for a second term as president, the internal problems between East and West Pakistan began to increase and came to the surface in many ways. The East Pakistanis felt they should have greater representation in the National Assembly because of their larger population. They also felt they were not well protected because the greater bulk of the Pakistani army was concentrated in West Pakistan. One of the reasons for this was the continuing dispute with India over the Kashmir issue. These feelings, coupled with the insistence that English was to be the official language, resulted in severe riots during the late 1960's. Ayub Khan was forced to retire in 1971 and was replaced by Agha Muhammad Yahya Khan. Once again Pakistan was placed under martial law as Yahya Khan struggled with the problems.

Since the major uprisings had occurred in East Pakistan, under martial law, troops, mainly West Pakistanis, were sent into East Pakistan to put down the uprisings. Because of the inability of the army to control the rebellious East Pakistanis under normal martial law, it began a systematic program of terrorism in early 1971. The result was the loss of tens of thousands of lives and brought about an open revolt against the West Pakistan government. More serious, it also brought India into the conflict on the side of the East Pakistanis, or Bengalis, after millions of them had fled to India to escape the slaughter of intellectuals and professional people. The result was the defeat of West Pakistan forces and the creation of the new nation of Bangladesh. (The background of Bangladesh and its painful creation will be examined in the concluding sections of this chapter.)

In Search of Stability. A new constitution was adopted in April 1973 and went into effect in August. It provided for a bicameral legislature: the National assembly with 200 members, having political power; and the Senate with ten members from each of the four provinces, three from the centrally administered tribal area and two from the federal capital area. Chaudhri Fazal Elahi became President and Ali Bhutto Prime Minister. The people opposed the government's enforced land distribution and nationalization of industry. When elections were held in March 1977 nine opposition groups formed the Pakistan National Alliance. Bhutto's party won the election, whereupon charges of corruption were levied. General Muhammad Zia-ul-Haq, chief martial administrator, was appointed head of a new civilian regime and Ali Bhutto was arrested and later executed. General Zia became President in September 1978. Political instability continues to plague the government of Pakistan, as well as its Muslim neighbors, Afghanistan and Iran.

C. THE GEOGRAPHIC AND CULTURAL BACKGROUND OF PAKISTAN

Although part of the subcontinent of India, the many differences in culture, language, and religion, set Pakistan apart from Bangladesh and India.

Climate and Geography.   Most of Pakistan is mountainous or on a high plateau. The tall peaks of the Himalayas to the west and north of the Indus River, and the barren stretches of the Thar Desert to the east contrast with the cultivated plains in the valley of the river and its tributaries. The great Indus River, some 1,700 miles in length, rises in Tibet and together with its five major tributaries waters half of the land area of Pakistan. However, less than a quarter of this land is under cultivation. The average rainfall is only 10 inches a year, not enough for the country's agricultural needs. Therefore, irrigation works are necessary for farming. There are more than 75,000 miles of irrigation canals in Pakistan and the government is building more.

The climate of Pakistan varies considerably. In the northern regions it is chilly from autumn to spring. The summer months are hot everywhere. Rainfall is concentrated in the period from July to September when the monsoon from the Bay of Bengal, far to the east, arrives with some of its moisture left over. This period coincides with the flooding of the Indus River, when the snows melt in the mountains. As a result, the water supply of Pakistan is adequate for only about three months of the year. That is why an extensive irrigation system had to be developed.

Pakistan covers an area of about 310,000 square miles, slightly larger than the state of Texas. It is bounded on the north by Afghanistan, on the east by India, on the west by Iran, and to the south lies the Arabian Sea. There are two contrasting regions in Pakistan. In the east is an area of flat plains and in the west are found high mountains, including the Hindu Kush, hills, and plateaus. The nation is made up of the former British India provinces of Sind, Northwest Frontier and Baluchistan, and West Punjab. The capital is Islamabad and the largest city is Karachi.

Peoples. Pakistan was frequently invaded from the west through the passes in the Himalayas, especially the famous Khyber Pass in the Northwest Frontier Province. Its people are mainly of mixed Baluchi, Pathan, and Arab ancestry and differ markedly in customs, traditions, and languages although the Moslem religion is a common element for the majority.

The Baluchi, said to be the descendants of Arabs who landed on the coast before the end of the 7th century, are nomadic tribes. The Pathans, related to the Afghanistani, consist of many tribes, some of whom wander with their flocks of sheep and goats in search of pasture. Others are farmers who raise wheat and fruits. The Pathans are fierce fighters, and frequently quarrel with each other over water rights or the scarce and valuable farm lands. Other peoples who live in Pakistan include the Hunzas and Gilgitis, found in the north; the Punjabis in the eastern part of the territory; and the Sindhis, south of the Punjab.

Languages.   Many different languages are spoken in Pakistan. While they belong to the Indo-European family of languages and stem from Sanskrit, an ancient language of India, each is quite different from the others and is written in a different script. In Karachi, Urdu is the principal spoken and written language. Urdu is a mixture of old Persian and Hindi with the addition of Turkish and Arabic words. Urdu and English are the official languages and are taught in the schools. However, Pashti and Sindi are spoken by about 15 percent of the people and Punjabi by even more.

Pakistan, for many centuries the point of entry into the subcontinent of India, has been influenced by Arabic, Turkish, and European cultures. It was in the Indus River Valley at Mohenjo-Daro and Harappa that one of the earliest civilizations developed. The Aryans, who invaded this valley some 4,000 years ago and conquered the original inhabitants, left their mark on its present culture.

D.   AGRICULTURAL AND INDUSTRIAL PROGRESS

Agricultural and Industrial Products.   About 90 percent of the approximately 74 million Pakistani inhabitants (1979 estimate) are engaged in agriculture. Among the principal crops are wheat, cotton, sugar, and tobacco. Wool and leather goods are important sources of income and valuable exports.

Pakistan's considerable mineral resources provide many jobs and are also important exports. Sizable deposits of limestone and gypsum provide materials for cement plants. Chromite is an exportable mineral and graphite, rock salt, pottery clays and glass sands are abundant. Half the country's fuel supply comes from the coal mined in Pakistan. Natural gas fields have been discovered in Baluchistan and pipelines connect them to Karachi and Muetan. Oil has been found at Dhulan and intensive exploration promises further discoveries.

Land Reforms.   More than half the land in Pakistan was

163

In Pakistan, industrialization and urbanization proceed at a rapid pace. Above, the new industrial town of Iskanderabad has a cement factory, a penicillin plant and a sugar factory. Below left, city officials discuss plans for the development of Karachi, the industrial and economic center of the country. However, in some areas of Baluchistan, primitive plows are still in use. (All photos: United Nations)

farmed by tenant farmers. Some 6,000 large landowners controlled much of the land. The average farm owned by a peasant was less than four acres, too small to provide both food for his family and a cash income for necessities.

President Ayub Khan, after a report by a Land Reforms Commission for West Pakistan, adopted a program to redistribute the land. No person was allowed to own more than 500 acres of the 24 million acres of irrigated land, or 1,000 acres of unirrigated land. The state took over the surplus holdings and sold them to the peasants, preferably to the tenants on those same pieces of land. The old owners were compensated for the loss of their land; the new owners were expected to repay the cost of the purchase of the land over a 25-year period. Government-owned land was also divided and sold to the peasants. Money was loaned to the new owners for the purchase of equipment. Other laws protected tenant farmers against high rent and from being forced off the land when they were working it. Over two and one-half million acres of land were redistributed, and some 75,000 landless peasants were settled on family farms.

Irrigation. The importance of irrigation projects to the many parts of Pakistan which do not receive enough rainfall has led the government to improve such facilities. Many projects have been completed in recent years or are nearing completion. Over 12 million additional acres of land have been or will be brought under cultivation with the completion of these projects. The Food and Agriculture Organization of the United Nations continues to aid Pakistan in its efforts to extend the quantity and fertility of semi-arid farm land. However, subsistence farming remains the main occupation for 85 per cent of the population.

Hydroelectric power is being generated from many irrigation projects—power to operate the increasing number of factories in Pakistan and power to electrify the villages. The Pakistan government plans to bring electricity to a thousand villages each year.

Industrial Growth. Foreign aid from the West has been a major factor behind Pakistan's remarkable industrial progress.

The United States has contributed over $4 billion in economic and military assistance.

When independence came in 1947, there was very little industry in Pakistan. Although Pakistan raised much of the subcontinent's raw materials, the great majority of the processing and milling plants were in India. Today, the state owns and controls over 7,000 miles of railroads, tele-communications, and part of the air transport industry. Most other industry is in private hands and operates on a capitalistic profit basis.

In the 1970's the government under President Ali Bhutto developed a series of measures designed to secure a more just and equitable distribution of national resources in order to ensure the flow of foreign investment and external aid. He established a board of industrial management to carry out industrial reforms. Labor reforms were also instituted with an increase of labor at the management level.

E.   FOREIGN RELATIONS

The creation of India and Pakistan in 1947 caused many problems that grew out of the division of the assets of the subcontinent. Ultimately, most of the problems were settled by long negotiations. The settlement of some, such as the Kashmir boundary dispute (see page 142) are still being negotiated.

The India-Pakistan War of 1971 created many more problems and will have repercussions for years to come. The creation of the new nation of Bangladesh from what had been East Pakistan, will be a constant source of friction between India and Pakistan. The next section will examine some of these problems in greater detail.

Pakistan and Afghanistan. The border between Pakistan and Afghanistan cuts through the tribes living in that area. The Pathans in Pakistan are related to the Afghans. For years after its independence, Pakistan was pressured by Afghanistan to allow the Pathans to join their own people on the other side of the frontier. When Pakistan refused to consider this at all, Afghanistan stopped trading with Pakistan. It also broke off diplomatic relations and turned to the Soviet Union for military equipment and the use of Soviet ports to ship Afghan goods. Through the efforts of the Shah of Iran, acting as a mediator, the two countries resumed diplomatic relations in 1963.

In recent years, relations between the two countries have become strained, due in part to political instability in both nations.

Pakistan and China. When China invaded India in 1962, Pakistan noted that the bulk of India's armies remained near the Pakistan border and were not withdrawn to fight the invaders. The United States and Britain sent military supplies to the Indians which angered the Pakistanis who claimed that this aid would be used against them and not the Chinese. In 1962, Pakistan signed a border treaty with China which ceded 13,000 square miles of Pakistani-held Kashmir to China. China also agreed to support Pakistan's position on Kashmir and supported the Pakistanis in their wars with India in 1965 and 1971.

Relations with China improved during the 1970's. The Chinese agreed to finance a major industrial complex in 1975 and are currently viewed as an important ally.

Pakistan and the United States. The relations between Pakistan and the United States have been cordial since 1947, although the United States halted all aid to both Pakistan and India after their 1965 war. Each country has resented the aid given by the United States to the other. India, particularly, has cooled off in its relations because of the position the United States took in the 1971 war. To India, this placed the U.S. and China in the position of defending Pakistani aggression against India aiding the Bengali struggle for freedom.

In 1975 the American government lifted a ten-year embargo on the export of arms to Pakistan. This led to closer ties which had been developing since U.S. support of Pakistan in the Bangladesh civil war. The two governments have had some major disagreements over the past few years, particularly regarding Pakistan's attempt to become a nuclear power in south Asia.

Pakistan and the Future.   As a new nation just accepted into the United Nations in 1947, the future looked bleak for the newly created state of Pakistan. However, under the leadership and policies of Ali Jinnah, and later Ayub Khan, Pakistan became a respected member of the family of nations. Eventually, the budget was balanced and Pakistan exports and imports figured heavily in the world balance of trade.

Unfortunately, internal disputes with the eastern section of the country, so widely separated by India from the mainstream of government and the center of economic life, eventually resulted in civil war of ghastly proportions in 1971. With India entering the dispute, for reasons which we will read about in the next section, Pakistan was soundly defeated; East Pakistan declared itself the new nation of Bangladesh. For awhile in 1972 it seemed that the entire economic and political structure of Pakistan might collapse.

President Ali Bhutto, educated in the United States and England, imposed strict measures on the economy and the military. He reestablished relations with India and Bangladesh and in 1973 war prisoners were exchanged. Ali Bhutto's successor, Muhammad Zia-ul-Haq (called General Zia), proclaimed Pakistan a Muslim republic in 1978 and has continued the economic and political rebuilding of the nation.

F.   BACKGROUND TO BANGLADESH
INDEPENDENCE

Bangladesh, a nation created in 1971, was born out of bloodshed and brutal war. We have read in the previous sections of this chapter how the state of Pakistan was created in 1947 and divided into two widely separated sections. About the only common ground between the eastern and western sections was the Muslim religion. There was little else to hold the people together for they differed in every other respct. Their land was different; their languages were different; their pre-independence history was different.

One of the major problems that faced Pakistan throughout the nearly 25 years of its existence as East and West Pakistan was how to govern such a geographically widely separated nation. With the main seat of government in West Pakistan and the majority of its citizens living in East Pakistan, quarrels over representation and government reform arose almost from the beginning. In the east, the Awami League, composed of Bengalis who were interested in greater autonomy for their section, was created by Sheik Mujibur Rahman.

In December 1970, when East and West Pakistanis went to the polls to elect a new National Assembly, Awami League candidates received a clear majority—167 seats out of 313. The military government, under Ayub Khan, postponed convening the National Assembly. In March 1971, riots broke out throughout East Pakistan against the government. To make matters worse, in November, 1970, Bangladesh had been subjected to one of the greatest natural disasters of all time. A cyclone and tidal wave had hit the land and killed an estimated 600,000 people. The Bengalis felt that the central government was indifferent to their tragedy and was not supplying sufficient aid.

Martial law was again imposed in Pakistan and the army, largely West Pakistani, was sent to the East to put down the riots. What followed for the next nine months was probably one of the greatest bloodbaths in modern history as the army began a systematic slaughter of the Bengalis. Professional people and intellectuals especially were massacred. An estimated one million Bengalis were brutally killed in the ensuing conflict. Nearly 10 million people crossed the border to India to escape. Another 10 million were displaced within Bangladesh.

Finally, India which had officially recognized the state of Bangladesh on December 6, entered the conflict. In the two

CASE INQUIRY: U.S. Aid to Bangladesh

The following speech was made by Representative Herman Badillo of New York in the House of Representatives:

Mr. Speaker, during the brief but bitter fighting between India and Pakistan last month the world bore witness to the folly of the ill-conceived policy of the United States toward India and, particularly, toward the struggle for independence in East Pakistan. For months prior to armed hostilities the United States stood mute and failed to raise its voice against the reign of terror perpetrated against the Bengalis of East Pakistan by Punjabis from the West. While it is true that this was an internal struggle, this country or any other member of the family of free nations simply cannot ignore or condone the blatant violation of basic human rights and dignity which occurred in Bengal or the snuffing out of lives of men, women, and children at the whim of some brutal dictator. The acts of genocide committed in East Pakistan demanded that a hue and cry of protest be raised, yet this nation remained silent. . . .

Mr. Speaker, time is long past due that the United States reassess its policy, both toward India and Bangladesh, and candidly admit its mistakes. By pursuing our present attitudes toward these two nations we have lost the faith of freedom loving people throughout the world and are ignoring some of the basic principles upon which our own country was founded. I wholeheartedly support legislation which has been introduced extending the immediate recognition of the United States to Bangladesh and the official acknowledgement that this is an independent nation.

We must, therefore, enact legislation providing for immediate emergency aid to Bangladesh to help it overcome the devastation wrought by the war and to assist this new nation in effectively coping with its many economic and social problems.

1. If you were a member of Congress and the official position of our nation was that the war in Pakistan was essentially a civil war, would you advocate U.S. intervention? Why?

Congressional Record, Thursday, January 27, 1972

weeks that followed, Indian and Bengali forces defeated the Pakistani troops. The losses in terms of people and damage to farmlands and industry were tremendous but the Bengalis were determined to rebuild their country and faced the future with new hope and dedication.

G. GEOGRAPHIC AND CULTURAL BACKGROUND OF BANGLADESH

Geography and Climate. Bangladesh has a land area of about 144,000 square miles, roughly the size of the state of Wisconsin; its population of 85 million makes it one of the most densely populated countries in the world. Most of the country is fertile land and river delta. Flood damage can be devastating during the monsoon season as it was most recently in 1978. The major agricultural products are jute, rice, and tea. Some of the largest jute mills in the world are located in Bangladesh.

Climate ranges from cool dry winters to tropical wet summers. The average rainfall is over 100 inches a year so there is no extensive need for irrigation projects as in Pakistan.

Peoples. The people of Bangladesh are said to be the descendants of the Dravidians, the earliest inhabitants of India, who were conquered by the Aryans. A large portion of the Bengali people were converted to Islam during the Arab invasion of India. The nation was continuously subordinated to other areas. Under British rule the region which is now Bangladesh was a part of the hinterland of Calcutta. In the late 19th century, the British began favoring Muslims for educational and governmental positions because of the growing Hindu-oriented nationalism. However, the Muslim middle class was not able to overcome the well-established advantage of the Hindus.

In 1947, when the area was placed under the control of the Muslim government of West Pakistan, the Bengali majority resented its lack of power. The Eastern province of Pakistan provided nearly two-thirds of the country's exports and trade revenues, yet the needs of the people were often ignored by government leaders in West Pakistan. After unsuccessful protests by Bengali leaders in 1968 and 1969, the civil war broke out in the following year. The war took a tremendous toll on the people of Bangladesh and recovery has been a slow and painful process.

Social Life.   At the end of the civil war, the Bengali society was shorn of the non-Bengali governmental and economic elite from the Western province. However, many Bengali professionals and intellectuals had been executed or killed during the conflict. Opportunities were now available for advancing into the empty positions including high government offices as well as leadership of major industries. During the 1970's the Bengalis have risen to positions of influence and power in the cities and countryside.

The role of women is still restricted. In the rural areas in particular, women rise in status and respect in their husbands' household as they give birth to sons. *Purdah* (the seclusion of women) can be found in many villages. Segregation of the sexes even exists in social groups who have accepted modern Western cultural practices.

Cultural Life.   The Bengalis are proud of their cultural heritage —including their language, forms of artistic expression, and religious background. The people have a reputation as being musical and poetic and this is reflected in their literature and poetry. Their strong national identity and sense of pride was a determining factor in the struggle to achieve independence.

The art and music of the Bengali people illustrates their close relationship with the land. The influence of the Hindu, Buddhist, and Muslim religions is also apparent. The architecture in the cities shows the British influence, similar to the colonial experience of India. The government's support of education and the arts is indicative of the national commitment to the culture of the people.

The performing arts—dance, the theater, and music—are firmly rooted in the history of the people. The impact of radio and television has spread rapidly in the past few years. Movies are also a popular form of entertainment.

Bangladesh's largest export and mainstay of the economy is jute. At top left, freshly harvested jute is prepared for its journey to Dacca, where it is made into cloth at one of the world's largest jute factories (top, right). Below, workers prepare jute bales for export. (All·photos: United Nations)

H. THE GOVERNMENT OF BANGLADESH

Sheik Mujibur Rahman.   Sheik Mujibur Rahman (Mujib) was the moving force in the Bengali independence movement. Shortly after the West Pakistanis invaded East Pakistan in March, 1971, Mujib was captured and imprisoned in West Pakistan. He was held in solitary confinement for nine months and, after Pakistan's defeat, was released by President Bhutto. Mujib returned to his country to find it in shambles.

Bangladesh began its existence with not much more than $500,000 in foreign exchange. The problems of rebuilding the torn nation were staggering. Putting a new government together was the top priority. Mujib, who had been named president while still in prison, adopted a provisional constitution for the state in 1972, naming a new cabinet with Abu Sayed Choudhury as president and himself as prime minister. He arranged a 25-year treaty of friendship and a trade treaty with India and then proceeded to nationalize various industrial and financial institutions. The United Nations and India provided food aid to avoid a famine. Bangladesh was quickly recognized by most nations.

The Constitution of 1972 was approved by the Constituent Assembly in November 1972. It provided for a single-chamber parliament with three hundred members elected by direct, universal adult suffrage and an additional fifteen women to be elected by the 300 members. As a result of the elections of March 1973 Sheik Mujib's party won an overwhelming victory, gaining 292 of the 300 seats. In 1973, President Choudhury resigned unexpectedly because of the limited powers of the office. He was succeeded by Muhammad Ullah, the former Speaker of the Parliament who was officially elected in January 1974.

Reconstruction.   The nation's reconstruction effort went forward slowly but steadily until the worst floods in two decades crippled the nation during July and August 1974. Bangladesh had to seek aid from other nations. The food supply was not sufficient for the nation's needs until 1976. Industrialization continued to increase

174

although at a rate below the stated goals. The economy was still sluggish, and the currency was devalued in May 1974.

The government continued to suffer from an inability to maintain law and order. A state of emergency was declared in December 1974 followed by a presidential regime. Sheik Mujib became President and served until he was overthrown and killed in August 1975. Khandakar Mushtaque Ahmed, known as Mushtaque, was sworn in as President. Pakistan was the first nation to recognize the new government, and formal diplomatic relations between the two nations were resumed.

Mushtaque was in turn forced to resign in November 1975, as part of a power struggle with the top command of the Army. Chief Justice of the Supreme Court Abu Sadat Mohammed Sayem then became President. Under his leadership the economy began to improve. The nation was fortunate in having a record harvest for 1975-76. Relaxation of some martial law aspects were indicated when the government permitted indoor meetings of political parties beginning in late July 1976.

The Zia Regime. In November 1976, Major General Ziaur Rahman (Zia) became chief martial law administrator. He became President after Abu Sadat Sayem resigned because of ill health. In a referendum in May 1977, an overwhelming majority approved the martial law regime, confirmed Zia as President and approved his 19-point program committing the nation to Islam, restoring democracy, and promising economic and social progress and justice for the nation.

General Zia began a rural development program in order to gain support for his economic policies. The self-help scheme was based on reducing the number of unemployed people which was estimated at between 6.9 and 9.7 million. His reconstruction program has helped to foster economic growth. He also continued the political reform program, removing the bans on political activities and holding a presidential election in June 1978 in which he was overwhelmingly reelected. He continued to relax martial law by reducing press censorship, releasing political prisoners and permitting public meetings.

Bangladesh and the Future. Bangladesh is not the only new nation to begin its life against tremendous odds. It has been accepted into the British Commonwealth of nations, which opens many doors in international trade and banking. In Dacca, the capital city of over one million people, the Indians, Americans, and Soviets are very much in evidence. Most are members of aid delegations, there to administer aid from their countries and to help the Bengalis continue to grow. The Soviets had helped to clear the harbor at Chittagong, the second largest city of Bangladesh. American aid has amounted to over $300 million—more than Soviet aid but not as much as India has provided. Bangladesh was admitted to the United Nations in 1974.

Perhaps the time has come when the subcontinent of India can build and develop itself economically and politically. One of the greatest problems of the partition following World War II now seems to be resolved; that is, people are living in ethnic groups rather than being subdivided solely on the basis of religion. Perhaps now these three relatively new nations, comprising nearly one-fourth of the world's population, will begin achieving their potential and lead Asia into the mainstream of world affairs.

QUESTIONS AND ACTIVITIES

MULTIPLE CHOICE TEST

In each of the following, you have three choices. Choose the only correct answer.
1. A major Asiatic country that was divided into two parts prior to 1971, each 1,000 miles from the other is (*a*) India, (*b*) Indonesia, (*c*) Pakistan.
2. Most of the people in Pakistan are (*a*) Muslims, (*b*) Hindus, (*c*) Sikhs.
3. The monsoons bring an abundance of rain to (*a*) Pakistan, (*b*) Bangladesh, (*c*) Kashmir.
4. The highest mountains on the Indian subcontinent are located in (*a*) Bangladesh, (*b*) India, (*c*) Pakistan.
5. One major difference between Bangladesh and Pakistan is (*a*) religion, (*b*) language, (*c*) methods of transportation.

176

6. The chief language spoken in Bangladesh is (*a*) Bengali, (*b*) Urdu, (*c*) Hindi.
7. A very early world civilization developed in the (*a*) Indus Valley, (*b*) Brahmaputra region, (*c*) southern part of India.
8. Rice is grown mainly in Bangladesh because of (*a*) the mountainous region, (*b*) adequate rainfall, (*c*) use of machinery.
9. The chief language spoken in Pakistan is (*a*) Urdu, (*b*) Hindi, (*c*) Bengali.
10. The first president of Pakistan was (*a*) Liaquat Ali Khan, (*b*) Muhammed Ali Jinnah, (*c*) Sir Said Ahmad Khan.
11. The Muslim League refused to support the Indian Congress Party because it (*a*) favored a separate state for Muslims, (*b*) wanted majority control in a united India, (*c*) did not want to separate from Britain.
12. At the time of partition, most of the subcontinent's manufacturing plants were (*a*) given to the Muslims, (*b*) kept by the British, (*c*) turned over to the Hindus.
13. The present president of Pakistan is (*a*) Muhammad Zia-ul-Haq, (*b*) Ali Bhutto, (*c*) Ali Jinnah.
14. The first government of Bangladesh was democratic under a parliamentary form modeled after that of (*a*) Burma, (*b*) England, (*c*) India.
15. Bangladesh has one of the greatest population densities per square mile (*a*) on the subcontinent of India, (*b*) in Asia, (*c*) in the world.
16. Land reform in Pakistan has *(a)* been opposed by the middle-class industrialists, *(b)* limited the size of farms, *(c)* not been very successful.
17. The Awami League of East Pakistan opposed the government in West Pakistan because (*a*) it wanted more representation, (*b*) it wanted to unite with India, (*c*) it championed women's rights.
18. The people of Bangladesh are said to be the descendants of (*a*) early Arabs, (*b*) early Mongolians, (*c*) early Dravidians.
19. The present leader of Bangladesh is (*a*) Ali Jinnah, (*b*) Khandakar Mushtaque Ahmed, (*c*) Ziaur Rahman.
20. Pakistan's foreign policies in recent years have brought it into closer relations with (*a*) India, (*b*) Afghanistan, (*c*) Communist China.
21. Because some of the tribes living in Pakistan are related to tribes in another country, bad feelings have broken out between Pakistan and *(a)* India, *(b)* Afghanistan, *(c)* the Soviet Union.
22. Bangladesh is not a member of *(a)* the United Nations, *(b)* the British Commonwealth, *(c)* the Muslim League.

KEY WORDS OR PHRASES

Can you explain the meaning and importance of the following names or phrases?

Khyber Pass
Urdu
Muhammad Ali Jinnah
Pathans
Mohammed Iqbal
jute
Sheik Mujibur Rahman
Kashmir
East Pakistan
Ali Bhutto

Muhammad Zia-ul-Haq
Agha Muhammad Yahya Khan
Bengali
Basic Democracies
parliamentary government
martial law
Sanskrit
Indus River
Aryan
Ziaur Rahman

COMPLETION QUESTIONS

Complete the following sentences, finding the answers from the list of words or names above.

1. .... is the chief language spoken in Bangladesh.

2. .... was a famous Muslim writer who did a great deal to promote the idea of an independent Muslim state.

3. .... is an ancient language of India from which the Pakistani language stems.

4. .... is an area over which Pakistan and India have had several armed disputes.

5. .... is the most important crop in Bangladesh.

6. .... has begun to attack the economic problems facing Bangladesh.

7. The most important river system in Pakistan is the .... system.

8. One of the major differences between the people of India, Pakistan, and Bangladesh is that the Pakistanis and Bengalis belong to the .... religion.

9. One of the main entry points into India from the main continent of Asia has been through the ....

10. .... was the leader of Pakistan at the beginning of the 1971 war.

11. One of the chief agitators for Pakistani independence and separation from Great Britain was the ....
12. .... was the first Prime Minister of Pakistan.
13. .... was imposed throughout all of Pakistan following the riots in March, 1971.
14. Reconstruction efforts in Bangladesh were halted following .... during July and August 1974.
15. .... was overwhelmingly reelected as President of Bangladesh in 1978.

THINGS TO DO

1. Read a biography of Ali Jinnah and report to the class on his contributions to the independent Muslim state.
2. As a representative of a travel agency, write a description of the sights to see in Pakistan or Bangladesh and the places of major interest to visit.
3. If you live in a city large enough to have a variety of foreign restaurants, find out if there is a Pakistani one and what kind of food they serve.
4. Prepare a pictorial display of the peoples, industries, and geography of Pakistan or Bangladesh. Consult the indexes of *Life, Asia,* and the *National Geographic* magazines for sources.
5. Prepare a class debate on the topic: "The United States should continue its program of military aid to Pakistan."
6. If there are any Pakistani or Bengali people living in your town, perhaps going to a college or university near you, invite one of them to give a talk to your class on the Muslim religion or the culture of their country.
7. Prepare a report on the ancient area of Bengal before the arrival of the British and then how British influence became very strong there.
8. Write to the U.N. for the latest population information on the nations of the world and prepare a chart on the population of each country and the population density per square mile.
9. Prepare a list of questions you would ask President Zia of Bangladesh in a television or magazine interview. Focus on such topics as political reform, rural and economic development, and aims of Bangladesh's foreign policy.
10. See your librarian for a novel or collection of short stories by a Pakistani or Bengali author. Read the book and prepare a brief report for your class.

SELECTED BIBLIOGRAPHY

GENERAL REFERENCES

Brown, W. Norman. *The U.S. and India, Pakistan, and Bangladesh*. Cambridge, Mass., Harvard University Press, 1972.
Examines U.S. relations with the three nations of Indian subcontinent.

Choudhury, G. W., *India, Pakistan, Bangladesh and the Major Powers*. New York, The Free Press, 1975.
An in-depth assessment of foreign relations between the United States, China, the Soviet Union, and the nations of the Indian subcontinent.

Current History. April 1979, pp. 145-186.
A series of articles on the social, political, and cultural changes in the nations of the Indian subcontinent.

INDIA

Armstrong, R. G., *Sisters Under the Skin*. New York, 1964.
Travel in India through the eyes of an American woman.

Fersh, Seymour. *India and South Asia*. New York, Macmillan Co., 1965.
A good introduction. The author is a former Education Director of The Asia Society.

Fischer, Louis. *Life of Mahatma Gandhi*. New York, New American Library, 1950.
A well-written account of his life, with special emphasis on his ideas and influence.

Jacobson, D. W. "Purdah in India: Life Behind the Veil." *National Geographic*. August 1977, pp. 270-286.
A vividly illustrated article on the seclusion of women in India, which is also practiced in Pakistan and Bangladesh.

"Lost India; Last Empire: Photographs of Victorian India." *Newsweek*. July 19, 1976.
Impact of colonialism on India reflected in historic and contemporary photographs.

180

Nehru, Jawaharlal. *Toward Freedom*. New York, John Day Co., Inc., 1941.
An excellent autobiography by Gandhi's successor.

Schulberg, Lucille. *Historic India*. New York, Time-Life Books, 1968.
A well-written historical overview of India's past with emphasis on art, architecture, and cultural achievements.

PAKISTAN

Bolitho, Hector. *Jinnah: Creator of Pakistan*. New York, Macmillan Co., 1955.
An excellent biography of the nationalist leader.

Bhutto, Zulfikar Ali. *The Third World: New Directions*. London, Quartet Books, 1977.
Essays on the politics, government, and foreign relations of Pakistan by the former Prime Minister.

Siddiqui, Kalim. *Conflict, Crisis, and War in Pakistan*. New York, Praeger Publishers, 1972.
Analysis of the events leading to civil war.

BANGLADESH

"Another War in Asia: Who is to Blame." *Newsweek*. December 20, 1971.

"Bangladesh: Out of War a Nation is Born." *Time*. December 20, 1971.
On the scene coverage of the birth of Bangladesh.

Chatterjee, Basant Kumar. *Inside Bangladesh Today: An Eyewitness Account*. New Dehli, S. Chand, 1973.
The first years of independence as seen by a noted Bengali.

Johnson, Basil. *Bangladesh*. New York, Barnes and Noble Books, 1975.
An excellent survey of social, political, and cultural practices.

INDEX

colonies, foreign, in India, 138

Communist China, 1; attack on India, 141, 145-146; relations with India and Pakistan, 144-146, 167; revolt against, by Tibet, 145

Communist Party in India, 143

Community Development program, 110-111

Congress Patry, 89, 96, 115, 156; formation of, 81-82; split with Muslim League, 88

cooperatives, establishment of, 114

Cornwallis, Lord, 69

cow, sacred, 34

cremation, 10

Curzon, Lord, 83

Dalai Lama, of Tibet, 145

Dalhousie, Lord, 70

Damão, 65

dancing, Indian, forms of, 129

Darius, I, king of Persia, 51

Deccan plateau, 2, 3-4, 7, 19

Delhi, 16; sultanate of, 58

Desai, Moraji, 47, 96, 100, 148

dharma, 33, 38, 51

Discovery of India, Nehru, 98

Diu, 65

doctors, in India, 14

Dravidians, 11, 50, 54, 171

Dupleix, Joseph, governor of, Pondichéry, 66

"dyarchy," 83

East India Company, British, 65-66; French, 66

East Pakistan, partition, 155, 156, 157-158; revolt in, 161-162; and creation of Bangladesh, 166, 168; government of, 170

education, in India, 121-126, under British, 122-123; control of, 122-123; elementary, 123-124; secondary, 124; adult, 126; in Pakistan, 161, 164

Eightfold Path, the, 41

Elahi, Chaudhri Fazul, 161

"Enlightened One," Buddha, 41

European interest in India, 64-65

First World War, India, and the, 84

Five Year Plans, 108-114

food, religious customs, 15; problems, 114-115

forests, of India, 22-23

Four Noble Truths, the, 41

Fourteen Points, the, 83

French, in India, 138

Gama, Vasco da, 65

Gandhi, Mahatma, 36, 37, 84-87, 89, 91, 124, 137; early life, 84-85; methods, 86-87; death of, 91

Gandhi, Indira, 37, 47, 96-99, 131, 142, 144, 147, 149

"Ganga Mata," 10

Gautama, Siddhartha, 39, 51

Genghis Khan, 58

Ghats, 4, 7

Ghurkas, warrior class, 149

Gilgitis, of Pakistan, 163

Glimpses of World History, 98

Goa, 65; Indian seizure of, 138, 143

Gokhale, Gopal K., 82

Granth Sahib, the, 42

Great Mutiny, the, 71-72

Greeks, in India, 51, 52, 54

Gupta Dynasty, 54-56; downfall, 56

Guru (Great Teacher), Nanak, 42

harijans (Children of God), 85

Harsha, Gupta king, 55

Hastings, Warren, 69

Himalayan Mountain Area, 2-3

Hinduism, 29-38, 56, 150; sources of, 30-31; great stories about, 31-32; chief religious ideas, 33; religious practices, 34; caste system, 34-38

Hindustan (Industan), 9

Hirakud Dam, 114

Hume, Allan O., 81

Hunzas, of Pakistan, 163

Hyderabad, 17, 92

India, the land, 1-4; climate, 4-9; rivers, 9-10; people and languages, 10-14; villages and cities, 14-17, 20; youth, 20; agriculture, 17-21; mineral resources, 21-25; religions, 29-43; history of, 48-61; British in, 64-77; European interest in, 64-65; British expansion in, 65-70; British reforms in, 72-76; independence for, 81-100; growth of nationalism, 81; British government reforms in, 82; and the World War I, 83; role of Gandhi, 84-87; in World War II, 88; winning of independence, 89; partition of, 89; mass migrations from, 89-91; princely states and, 91-92; new states of, 92; government of, 92-94; individual liberties in, 94-95; voting in, 95; political parties in, 96; great prime ministers, 97-100; economic and social problems, 106-132; population problems, 115-116; industrial growth, 116-118; education in, 122-126; arts of, 128-129; role of women in, 130-131; in the world of nations, 137-151; policy of non-alignment, 137-138, 148; foreign colonies in, 138; relations with Pakistan, 140-142; relations with Soviet Union, 142-144; relations with Communist China, 144-146; and the United States, 146-149
India-Pakistan War, 99, 166
Indian National Congress, 87-89
Indo-American Foundation, 147
Indo-Aryan language, peoples, 11
industry, expansion of, 116-118; financing, 119; growth in Pakistan, 164-166
International Bank for Reconstruction and Development, 140
Iqbal, Mohammed, 156
Iron Pillar, the, 55
irrigation projects, 112
Islam, 38, 57; influence of, on Pakistan, 155-156; on Bangladesh, 171

Jahan, Shah, 60
Jainism, 38-39, 51
Jaipur, 17
jajmani, 14
Japan, production of rice, 21
Jesuit missionaries, 42
Jinnah, Muhammad Ali, 88, 89, 156-157, 158

Kalidasa, "Indian Shakespeare," 55
karma, 33, 51
Kashmir, 47, 91, 92, 141-142, 157, 160, 166, 167; partition of, 141; war over, 142, 161; peace treaty, 142
Kasim, Muhammad ben, 57
Kerala, Communists in state of, 143
Khan, Ali Liaquat, 157
Khan, Ayub, 142, 158, 159, 160, 165, 168, 169
Khrushchev, 143
Khyber Pass, 2, 59, 156
Koran, the holy book, 38
Kosygin, 143, 144
Krishna, the god, 31, 32
Kshatriyas, 36

land reform, in India, 111-112
Land Reforms Commission, 164-165
languages, of India, 10-14; of Pakistan, 164; of Bangladesh, 172
Law Book of Manu, the, 31
liberties, individual, 94-95
Lok Sabha ("House of the People"), 93

Macaulay, Thomas B., 122
Madras, 17
Mahabharata, 31, 50
maharajah, of Kashmir, 141; of Sikkim, 150
Mahavira, 39, 51
Mahmud of Ghagni, 57, 59
"Majra," by Khushwant Singh, 8

Malabar coast, 4
Manu, Law Book of, 31
manufacturing, in India, 25
Mao Tse-tung, 144
Marathas, the, 60
mathematics, Indians develop, 55
Maurya Empire, the, 52-54
minerals, of India, 21-22
Mirza, Iskandar, 158
Mogul Empire, the, 59-61; culture, 59-60; downfall, 60-61
Mohammed Iqbal, 156
Mohenjo-Daro, 9, 49, 163
moksha, 33
Mongols, 58
monsoon winds, 3, 6-9
Montagu-Chelmsford Reforms, 83
Morley-Minto Reforms, 82
Mountbatten, Lord Louis, 89
Muhammad, prophet, 38, 57
music, Indian, 130
Muslim League, 83, 88, 89; formation of, 156
Muslim period, 56-59
Mutiny, the Great, 71
Mutual Defense Assistance Agreement, between Pakistan and the U.S., 167
Mysore, Sultan of, 69

Nanak, Guru (Great Teacher), 42
nationalism, growth of, 81-83; weakness of Indian, 83-84; Gandhi's role, 84-88
Nehru, Jawaharlal, 89, 97-98, 137, 138, 144, 145
Nepal, 1, 146, 149-150
New Delhi, 16
nirvana, complete peace, 41, 51
non-alignment, India's policy of, 137-138, 147
non-cooperation, policy of, 86-88
Northwest Frontier Province of Pakistan, 163

"overseas provinces," Portuguese, 138

Pakistan, 1, 2, 58; war with India, 99; India's relations with, 140-142; history of, 155-156; partition of, 157-158; government of, 158-161; new constitution, 159-160; East Pakistan revolt, 160-161; climate and geography, 161-162; peoples, 162; languages, 162; agricultural and industrial products, 163; land reforms, 163-164; irrigation in, 164; industrial growth, 23, 165-166; relations with Afghanistan, 167; relations with China, 167; relations with U.S., 167; and the future, 167; and Bangladesh, 155-174
Panch Shila, 144, 145
Pandit, Mme. 132
Parsis, 43
Pathans, of Pakistan, 163
Pax Britannica, 73
Peacock Throne, 60, 61
peoples of India, 10-11
periods in Indian history, 48-61; prehistoric, 48-50; Hindu, 50-57; Moslem, 57-61
Persians, in India, 51
Plassey, Battle of, 67
polygamy, 130, 131
population, growth of, 115-116
Portuguese, in India, 65; lose Goa, 138
Praja Socialist Party, 95
princely states, and India, 91-92
Protestant missionaries, 42
Punjab, the, 42

Rahman, Sheik Mujubur, 169, 174-175
Rahman, Ziaur (Zia), 175
Raiya Sabha ("Council of States"), 93
rajahs, tribal chiefs, 50
Raman, Dr. C. V., Nobel Prize, 126
Ramayana, the, 31, 32, 50
Reddy, Neelam Sanjiva, 99-100
reincarnation, 33